I0021748

Lean Software Development

Avoiding Project Mishaps: A Guide Beyond the Basics

By

Gary Metcalfe

Copyright 2018 by Gary Metcalfe- All rights reserved.

The following book is reproduced below with the goal of providing information that is as accurate and reliable as possible. Regardless, purchasing this book can be seen as consent to the fact that both the publisher and the author of this book are in no way experts on the topics discussed within and that any recommendations or suggestions that are made herein are for entertainment purposes only. Professionals should be consulted as needed prior to undertaking any of the action endorsed herein.

This declaration is deemed fair and valid by both the American Bar Association and the Committee of Publishers Association and is legally binding throughout the United States.

Furthermore, the transmission, duplication or reproduction of any of the following work including specific information will be considered an illegal act irrespective of if it is done electronically or in print. This extends to creating a secondary or tertiary copy of the work or a recorded copy and is only allowed with express written consent from the Publisher. All additional right reserved.

The information in the following pages is broadly considered to be a truthful and accurate account of facts and as such any inattention, use or misuse of the information in question by the reader will render any resulting actions solely under their purview. There are no scenarios in which the publisher or the original author of this work can be in any fashion deemed liable for any hardship or damages that may befall them after undertaking information described herein.

Additionally, the information in the following pages is intended only for informational purposes and should thus be thought of as universal. As befitting its nature, it is presented without assurance regarding its prolonged validity or interim quality. Trademarks that are mentioned are done without written consent and can in no way be considered an endorsement from the trademark holder.

Table of Contents

Introduction

Congratulations on purchasing *Lean Software Development* and thank you for doing so.

The two terms "lean" and "Agile" have been used most often in reference to software development methodologies, organizational styles, and project management.

Well, do you ever find yourself confusing the two? Or maybe asking yourself questions like what is lean? What is agile? How are they different?

According to Merriam-Webster Dictionary, agile is defined as "possessing a quick and resourceful and adaptable character, or identified with the ability to move with rapidly".

On the other hand, lean is defined as "thin and healthy or having little or no fat".

Depending on the following definitions, you can make an assumption that an individual who is lean and another one who is agile have many shared characteristics. The same is true in the case of software development.

Today, there is an increased confusion of what is lean and what is agile. Discussions everywhere continue with some wanting to know whether it is one and the same, and which one should be applied.

Briefly, both Lean and Agile emerged because of the many problems that the Waterfall model had. Software engineers and developers started to notice some of the shortcomings of the Waterfall model in the 90s. With the increased dynamic in markets and tech-savvy users, the Waterfall model wasn't possible to live up to the market demands, to deliver a bug-free software on a regular basis.

As a result of the pursuit of a better model, the Lean and Agile creators focused on building a methodology that is more customer-focused. This book starts with a background of Lean software development. It will look at the origin, values, and principles of Lean. The subsequent chapters will explore deep into the concept of Lean and how it can be useful in software development.

Chapter 1: Background to Lean Software Development

Lean originated from Toyota's method of car manufacturing. The principle behind Toyota's method of car manufacturing is currently applied in the world today. As long as you apply the principles correctly, you'll for sure succeed. All principles are universal, although the specific practices may be different. Lean principles are constant and can't change no matter the time. However, Lean practices should be different as the environment changes from one place to another.

The principles that drive Lean can be used in the software development industry. This provides a means for those developers who want to create better software products. Since Lean principles have similar practices as agile, this chapter will discuss Lean depending on Agile practices. This will allow you to see how agile practices can be a blueprint of Lean principles. Lean principles show

how different things compare to how normal agile practices work. Once you make certain things explicit, experts in agile have the ability to improve the methods.

Lean is used in Many Different Levels of the Organization

An enterprise includes all parts of an organization that contributes to the value stream of the product or service. In an IT company, this may include both the business and IT section, while in a product company, this may include marketing, sales, development, and support.

Enterprises in Lean require a swift coordination of business, delivery teams, and management to make sure that there is a better product delivered. Additionally, this product should be based on the priorities of the business.

Quick Dive of Lean Principles

The main ideas of Lean are based on the following considerations:

- When there are a lot of errors and the development system has to be improved.
- Doing things early may generate waste.
- Principles of Lean require an individual to concentrate on shortening time-to-market by eliminating delays found in the development process using Just-In-Time methods.
- Respect people to improve the system

These are important principles because everything has to start from any of them.

Identify Sources of Errors in Your System

For many people, when things aren't going well, the usual response is to identify whom to blame. Take, for instance, if a plane crash happens, people will always want to know who was at fault. Was it the pilot or airline's fault? Or was it the mistake of the plane manufacturer? Well, it's not a good thing to look for somebody to blame.

In software development, let's say that you want to write a feature of an existing system. You'll be provided with a document prepared by an analyst. This document contains all the functions that you need to build. This means that as a developer, you have no chance to interrogate a person who could be using the software to understand something more about the software. Your role is to write the code and test it. After you are done with testing, the new features are delivered to the customer to look and give his or her feedback. Also, the customer has the right to reject the new features if he or she isn't happy.

Assume if a customer rejects the new features. Who will be the right person to blame? Do you blame the customer for not being clear? Or the analyst for failing to write a great document? Or you blame the tester for not testing it correctly? If you carefully reflect on this incidence, you should notice that there is no one to carry the blame.

Despite this, the source of the problem lies with the all the team members of the project. From this example, you can see that every individual seems to work separately in a particular role. This means that there is no room for feedback loops.

An agile methodology supports team collaboration. For this case, the customer, developer, analyst, and the tester meet in a central place to expand the needs of the customer. It is a better system because once errors are identified, the team starts to look for ways to fix the errors and improve the communication process.

To improve the status of communication is the main goal of agile development. Unfortunately, agile practices go wrong when it overemphasizes communication at the lowest level between teams and the customer. On the other hand, Lean practices allow the spread of communication in many different settings by focusing communication on the end-to-end value. This provides a similar ground for every individual involved. As a result, it becomes possible for different organization layers to work together, with the main purpose of continuous process improvement and early delivery. Lean thinking will support the elimination of waste and delays.

Show Respect to People

If you take the time to interact with the Lean methodology, you'll frequently come across the words "respect people". These words are simple but have a moral lesson that everyone should learn.

A company may fail to respect its employees but still be successful. There are some organizations that can treat their workers and clients without any respect but still remain profitable. However, the truth is that showing respect is not only a responsibility of the business but it is a great thing.

You can look around the internet and you'll discover that many studies show how respect is important. Companies that featured in the Fortune Magazine all have a way of working that respect their employees. The biggest lesson is that if you show people respect, then there's always a reward. You'll go to rest feeling rejuvenated because you improved the lives of others.

Respect is the reason why management and employee flexibility attracts successful people. In software development, respect involves teams respecting each other, as well as remaining responsible for the tasks they are meant to do. Additionally, it is by respecting people and being accountable to the processes that they should follow that helps them develop a better software. In other words, a process in software development is the main foundation by which a team can build the best software.

Unfortunately, although the precise application of the term "respect for people" may be less perfect. Leaders have a chance to experience less pressure that makes them decide to prioritize short-term gains. Or they may not really understand a better means of doing business.

Fortunately, the presence of a continuous improvement system has shown to be the best way to build a culture that respects the contributions of the teams and strengthens the organizations.

Limiting Complexity and Rework

One thing that is clear in the minds of all developers is to limit the complexity of work and avoid any rework. Clarity requires that you know how to eliminate waste. Although it's difficult to completely ignore rework and avoid complexity, principles of Lean can help limit the complexity.

Waste Elimination

It's the main goal of any Lean expert. In the software industry, waste is a code that is very complex than how it should be. Waste appears because of defects in a source code. It's an effort that doesn't add any value to the product.

Any time there is waste in the system, it is the role of the Lean developer to search in the system a way to eliminate the waste. Elimination of waste is the permanent solution. If you don't remove the waste, the error in the system will keep re-occurring in a different form until that moment when you fix the system that generated it.

Deferring Commitment

To defer commitment is to make the right decisions at the right time. In most cases, these decisions are made at the "last responsible moment". Don't fall into the trap and make early decisions when you don't have all resources or information. Similarly, don't wait for too long and make the decisions very late because this will increase the chances of getting higher costs.

To defer commitment is a pro-active way of planning a process to avoid making decisions that will require you to change later after you get additional information. You can choose to apply this principle during analysis, system design, and development.

Defer Commitment to Requirements and Analysis

Many people think commitment is making a decision or taking an action. Well, there is something more to commitment than that and you're going to learn here. First, commitment is also the amount of time you spent doing a particular thing. Once you spent your time to fix a bug, you can't revise that time, it's gone forever.

Therefore, in gathering software requirements, an important question to ask yourself is how well can you spend that time? Is it worthy enough to discuss everything with the customer? If you can answer these questions, then you'll be on the correct path. Of course, there are certain requirements that you don't need to discuss with your customers. Some are more important than others.

That is why it's advised to start with requirements that rank higher on the ladder and provide a lot of functions to the business.

Some of the requirements that may be important to a business include those that offer a better value to the customer. The agile approach manages this by performing a deep analysis of the requirements that customers might think it is important. This is why iterative development is critical in agile practices. An iterative development will help an individual to see the different kinds of risk that a given requirement may cause in case it's ignored.

Defer Commitment in Design and Programming

When designers encounter design problems, they always select one or two approaches, though, they aren't sure. One way is by selecting the easiest things without caring about the future requirements. Another way is to anticipate some of the things that might happen and install hooks into the system for specific responsibilities.

In either way, there are challenges. The first approach will lead to a type of code that is hard to change. This happens because it's difficult to consider the dynamic nature of the code when you write it. On the other hand, the second approach will generate that is more complex. This is true because software developers have no time to predict how the future will be. Thus, if they have some anticipation how a specific system may work in future, they install hooks that appear to add complexity to the system.

A more different approach to these two approaches is called "emergent design". Emergent design in software industry requires three types of disciplines:

- Limit the implementation of design patterns to current features alone.

- Use the thought process of design patterns to build an application architecture that is flexible and resilient.

- Write automated acceptance.

If you apply the standard design patterns in the software industry, your code becomes easy to change. If you can limit the code you write to what you want currently, it will reduce the complexity of your code. An automated testing will change the design and make it even better. If you put into consideration all the aspects of emergent design, you'll know how to defer commitment of a specific implementation until the time when you make your mind about what you should do.

Using Iterative Development to Limit Complexity and Rework

The most popular causes of complexity include:

- Writing code that is not needed.

- Writing a tightly coupled code.

Iterative development helps a developer to write only useful code. In other words, the focus of iterative development is to help a developer identify what the customer wants and avoid creating things that add no value to the customer. Emergent design is great to decouple code without having any complexity in the process.

Create Knowledge

Knowledge is important in an agile process. Knowledge is created in a step wise manner in agile processes to help discover the exact thing that the customer wants to create or build. Once you have done that, you'll be able to deliver a quick value and avoid producing things that have a lower value.

Software development is like a journey of self-discovery than a building process. Software on its own has a minimum value. However, value comes through the kind of products and services delivered. Therefore, it's better to think of software development as a means by which you develop a product. In brief, it consists of a set of activities that you can use to discover and produce products that suit the needs of customers.

If you consider it this way, then it's clear that the purpose of software in IT organizations is to support a company's products and services. For software companies, software exists as a way to boost the work and needs of the customers. Software is the road that leads to an end. The end describes the type of value it adds to the customer. This can be direct or indirect. For that reason, you should consider software development as a step in product development.

Product development features these three steps:

1. Discover the needs of the customer.

2. Determine how to build it.

3. Build it

In the software development, time is spent in the third stage. However, the first two steps take more time. Let's assume that you are done with a software development project, then something happens that causes you to lose all your source code. In case you want to build the same system again, how long can that take you? Some developers may say that it may take them 20 to 50 percent of the previous time. Well, then a good question to ask is what is it that you did in the other 50 or 80 percent of the time?

The truth is that you spent this time in an attempt to find out the customer needs and determine how you can build that.

Creating knowledge requires that you master each process that you used to build the software. Once you master the methods, then there is no big deal on how you should improve it.

Deliver Early and Regularly

If you want to impress a customer and win their hearts, then the secret lies with early delivery. Early delivery means that there is a better market penetration, deep credibility of the business, and strong royalties. In addition, this generates early revenue to support the initial product release to pay for subsequent development.

This lean principle is also called "deliver fast". However, it's okay for you to think of it as a way of removing delays. If you didn't know, delays are a type of waste. This means that once you remove delays in your system, you'll immediately start to deliver early to all your customers. Despite this, don't forget that the main focus is to produce better value for the customer. The best value is one that has no delays at all. Therefore, if you can remove any delays, everything is going to move faster. Even your customers will start to smile. While there are great benefits that come when you deliver a product or service fast, it's advised to do it a way that is sustainable.

Build Quality

It's always hard to maintain the marks or standards of development. In fact, software companies that continue to thrive because of the quality of their service and product put so much effort. Employees are all trained to adhere to the best standards that have been set. Therefore, to mirror the same standards in your company or organization, you'll first need to train your teams rigorously to learn how to enforce quality in the code they write.

Once the standards of quality are implemented in a process, it becomes easy to identify waste and remove it from the process. One way of achieving this is by performing acceptance tests before you write the code. These types of tests are important because it allows the developer to gain some insights into the function of the system and requirements that should be implemented.

Also, you can improve the quality of the code by applying methods of eliminating waste. Many developers take time to find out how to fix bugs reported by customers. Without automated testing, errors will arise. A poorly written code is difficult to understand and leads to waste.

Optimize the Whole

One of the main changes in Lean thinking is to forget the belief that you need to optimize each step. However, if your goal is to increase the efficiency of the production process, you should concentrate on improving the value from the start of the production cycle until the end. Thus, if you only increase the efficiency of each machine, it will not improve the efficiency of the whole production flow.

The problem that comes with optimizing each step is that it produces large inventories between every step. In the software industry, "inventories" represent work that has been done partially. This type of work is yet to be designed, coded, or even tested.

However, Lean has proven that a single piece of flow is more effective than concentrating on finishing things fast. Inventories will deal with errors found in the process. In the physical world, this is represented by construction errors. In a software environment, this can deal with a misunderstanding that exists with the customer, or integration errors, but not any number of other things.

The Fast-Flexible Flow

The goal of lean is to optimize the whole. This is well summarized by the words "fast-flexible-flow". This requires you to adopt an idea into the development pipeline and channel it out to the customer quickly. When you remove the challenges found in this type of flow, it improves the whole process. Remember, it's the purpose behind the agile practice of creating a single story at a time. It requires that you have a customized code, design, and testing done towards the end of each iteration. It's something like, "This is what I have done, this is what I am going to do, and these are my challenges".

Concentrate on Time

To produce any item in large quantity, then you have to invest heavily on the machine. Despite this, Lean is concerned more on time instead of how well you're using resources. Lean requires everyone to limit the time taken to shift from a single idea to something substantial. In fact, Lean recommends for one to move faster by improving the efficiency of the process. This will cause costs to go down because there is a better quality with few errors and minimum waste. Unfortunately, if you concentrate so much on cutting down costs, it will not increase quality or speed.

When it comes to Lean, the goal is to reduce the waste of delays in software development. Examples of popular delays include:

- The interval between when a requirement is defined until when it's verified to be correct.

- The time between when a code is written until it's tested.

- The time taken for a customer to respond to the analyst or developer.

All these delays are a form of waste. It's a type of waste that happens when something wrong multiplies as the delay increases. When factor in all these delays, you'll start to see the reason why the way resources are utilized is a wrong approach.

Many people work on multiple projects simultaneously, either because they are waiting for other resources or information. For instance, if a developer sends an e-mail to an analyst and waits for a response, chances are that the developer will have another project at hand to work on. This is one of the causes for why developers work on many projects at the same time. Multitasking is a difficult process because it causes delays in communication and completion of tasks on time.

In the manufacturing industry, Lean provides a solution to this problem by creating work cells that control individual process and maintain their work by extracting a queue of prioritized activities.

Reflections on Just-in-time (JIT)

In a traditional software model, you first have to select all the requirements and start to build each requirement step-wise. All resources that teams need are made available at different stages. Since you'll be building many things at once, it's important to make a great effort and determine whatever it's that you need to do before you can begin the manufacturing process. For a JIT, you are supposed to deal with the items that you require and only before they are requested. This resembles the agile practice of selecting a story and doing an analysis just before it's developed.

If you can work in small steps, JIT in the software industry will provide the ability to change the direction before each energy in the process ends. One of the main things about Lean manufacturing is to limit-work-in process. Agile methods focus on this too.

In general, if you want to realize an easy JIT, then you should ensure that you have a smooth, low-error rate process. This kind of requirement makes sure that if there are any defects in the process, it should be easy to notice.

The just-in-time approach has many other advantages. Apart from revealing problems in the processes, it also shows problems that exist in the production. For example, in mass production, many errors are identified only in the final stages of production. If there is a huge inventory between steps, bad inventory will have to be produced before you can identify any error. In a software environment, a delay in detecting an error may result in a wasted effort to develop and test a code. In addition, this adds to the complexity of the system even if it doesn't create any value for the customer.

Essentially, if you can deploy a complete code to a customer and in small chunks, it's then possible to get feedback and determine whether you're creating something valuable. In summary, JIT acts a guide in software development. Think of agile practices as a type of JIT principle. No need to analyze a story fully before you build it. It's important to first analyze, design, write code, and test before each stage, this will help you uncover challenges that exist in the process. The just-in-time approach creates time to build things in small steps and supports the idea of rapid feedback from the customer.

Value Stream Mapping

These are a set of actions that add value to a customer. The addition of value starts from the time the first request was made to the last point it was delivered. Value stream begins with the original idea, moves through different states, and it reaches the final delivery.

The map of a value stream includes a Lean tool that experts select to apply in the value stream. Mapping of a value stream is done by using different pictures to show the process streams and use it to search for waste. The goal is to improve the total time from start to end of the entire stream while you maintain the future pace.

One of the key benefits of a value stream map is that it describes the entire picture. Many Agile users focus on raising the performance status of the team. But in many cases, the team may not trigger the development of challenges, even when it seems so. The map of a value stream shows how one can successfully optimize the whole by detecting waste and other factors that can affect the quality and slow the delivery.

Chapter 2: Value Creation and Types of Waste

In the lean industry, the value of a product depends on what the customer wants and is ready to cash out. Operations in productions are classified into the following three activities:

- Value-added activities

- Necessary non-value added.

- No value added activities.

Value-added activities change the type of product that the customer wants. Manufacturing is a physical change of a product that ensures expectations of a customer are fulfilled. Lean manufacturing will identify waste found in a value-added activity. Most importantly, it will limit pure non-added activities that have a huge effect on lead-time. This shows that Lean eliminates waste and optimizes activities that produce value from the customer's perspective. As a result, waste elimination is the basic principle of Lean manufacturing.

Types of Wastes

The "seven wastes" is among the most significant continuous improvement phrases you will hear all the time. Most of the lean tools, at their key point, concentrate on eliminating waste to enhance the flow.

There are seven wastes that Lean manufacturing identifies. These wastes outline a systematic procedure to classify problems and highlight areas that need improvement. When you are inspecting a process, looking for the seven wastes will allow Lean teams to find more chances that they can use to streamline the flow of work.

The 7 Wastes

- Defects

- Motion

- Over-processing

- Waiting

- Overproduction

- Transportation

- Excess inventory

Taiichi Ohno is credited as the father of Lean. He identified overproduction as the worst of all the 7 wastes. Now, there is an extra waste that should be added to the original seven wastes. This 8th waste is referred to as creativity. Don't be carried away on classifying the type of waste something is. No matter which type you assign it to. If something is Muda, remove it, as much of it as possible.

In the Lean culture, waste is defined as anything that doesn't add value. Keep in mind the term waste is often used interchangeably with the Japanese word, Muda, but more precisely, Muda refers to "wasteful activity". It is somehow related to the term mura that means variation or inconsistency.

These 7 types of wastes were chosen to be part of the Toyota Production System. However, they have widely been used by different experts in Lean.

1. Overproduction

If you produce more products than what you can handle or even produce something early than when it was needed, then that is considered overproduction. It's a form of waste because it's going to increase the risk of producing a wrong item and selling them at a discount. Still, there are situations where more produce of semi-finished products can be handled by Lean manufacturers.

Overproduction is ranked as the worst types of waste because it affects the smooth flow of goods and also affects the quality of the products. Furthermore, it affects quality and productivity. Since it's hard to detect problems early, products can depreciate in quality and the rate may not be generated. In addition, this may cause more work-in-process that might lead to a physical disruption of activities. Other effects of overproduction include extra equipment, inventory stockpiles, unbalanced workflow, batch processing, extra floor space, and hidden problems.

2. Defects

Besides the physical defects that affect the prices of goods sold, errors may also occur in the paperwork, late delivery, and use of many raw materials in the production process.

Defects require one to perform a rework. If not, the product is deleted. Producing products with defects will not only waste material and labor resources, but it will also cause shortages, produce idle time at different workstations, and extend the manufacturing lead time. Defects cause extra tools, additional manpower, missed delivery, and low profits.

3. Inventory

A waste inventory is one with a higher level of raw materials, finished products, and work-in-process. Excess inventory leads to better financial costs, increased rate of defects, and increased cost of storage. Inventory increases the lead time and discourages communication. To do a great purchase, first, you must clear the inventory because of the wrong lead times and due-dates. The elimination of buffer stock is a problem that should be addressed. Some of the effects of inventory include extra space, complex rework, and long lead time.

4. Transportation

This refers to the movement of materials that have no value to the product. It can be the movement of materials between workstations. The idea behind moving materials between production stages should concentrate on the output of the process. The movement of materials between processing stages goes past the production cycle time, inefficient application of labor and space. When examined carefully, any type of movement can be defined as waste. That is why it is advised to reduce the distance of movement instead of eradicating it completely. In addition, more movements may damage and affect the communication distance of every process. Examples of waste that occurs from transportation include multiple storage locations, excess material, wrong inventory counts, and complex inventory management.

5. Waiting

It's the idle time caused by workers and machines. Waiting happens because of insufficient production flow in the factory. Furthermore, waiting has some little delays between the units of processing. Waiting has negative effects because the cost of labor increases.

If you use time in the right way, then there will be no waste because of waiting. This waste happens when goods fail to move or developed. Waste that is caused by waiting affects products, workers, and goods. Waiting time for workers can be best used to train or control activities. However, it should not lead to overproduction. The effect of waiting is unbalanced operations, unplanned equipment downtime, and many more.

6. Motion

Any irrelevant physical motions that affect the attention of workers from doing their actual work is a form of waste. For example, workers walking around the factory floor to look for a tool or a difficult physical movement caused by a poorly designed ergonomics that will reduce the speed of workers.

Some of the waste in motions include poor ergonomics of production. This type of waste is likely to cause poor productivity and affect the quality of problems. Waste from motion may also cause poor management and tools to go missing.

7. Overprocessing

It happens when you intentionally do more processes than what the customer wants depending on the quality of the product and features of the application.

Overprocessing takes place in cases that involve complex solutions. The over-complexity causes employees to overproduce. A more complex solution may have extra transportation and features poor communication. Furthermore, overprocessing has many different kinds of problems. Some of those problems include the absence of a clear customer specification, redundant approvals, and excess information.

Sources of wastes are related to each other, thus, if you eliminate one source of waste, it will help reduce other sources. However, an important type of waste is the inventory. Completed parts and work-in-process don't add any value to a product and it's important for it to be eliminated. Once you limit an inventory, it becomes easy to take any actions. Elimination of waste is a great step for survival in the modern world. Organizations have to try and build a high-quality and low-cost product that reaches the customer quickly.

That said, there are several tools and techniques that Toyota developed to use to limit the source of waste. Some of those tools include:

Lean Manufacturing Tools and Techniques

When a company identifies the main sources of waste that they seem to produce, they can choose to use available tools that will help them make the right action so that they can eliminate the waste. Below are some of those tools that a company, individual, or organization can use.

1. Cellular Manufacturing

The main advantage of cellular manufacturing is realized when the cellphones are developed, controlled, and operated just in time. A successful application of the manufacturing cells requires one to deal with the selection, design, and operation. Selection involves choosing types of machines of a given cell.

Cell design involves layout description, production, and handling of requirements. How a cell works require an individual to define the number of operators and the type of operator that is in control. Finally, there is a cell control that has methods that one can use to measure the performance of a cell. The layouts of a cell are determined by the following features.

- **Continuous flow:** In this type of flow, the flow is said to be smooth. All components flow without any obstruction.

- **One-piece flow:** In this type of flow, only a single product will pass through the manufacturing process at a time.

- **Multi-purpose workers:** In this case, only one worker can be present in each cell. This is different from the batch processing where workers are responsible for a single process. In the case of cell manufacturing, workers have been given permission to be accountable for each unique process that happens in the cell. This means that each worker goes through a short training to deal with every process that happens in the cell.

- **U-shape:** The cells have a U-shape. The product changes from one side of the U as it is processed. Its function is to reduce the distance and the way materials travel inside a cell. The layout of a cell may cause a person to discover many lean objectives because of its ability to remove non-value-added activities from the production process.

2. Standardization of Work

This is a major principle of waste elimination. A standardized work will ensure that each task is arranged and handled in the most effective manner. This requires that the production process and guidelines are well defined and communicated. By doing so, it removes doubts and wrong assumptions. The focus is that the production has to be dealt in the same way every time. Just in case the production process isn't standardized, the workers may require to apply a different set of ideas. An advanced process of standardization means that the company can expand the capacity without any issues.

In lean manufacturing, a standard work has different key elements:

- **The standard of work sequence:** The sequence that an employee should follow to perform a task. This sequence is well defined to reduce variation and defects. It's a complex process because it illustrates each single hand movement by the worker.

- **Standard timing**: Takt time is the frequency that a single piece is released. This is the rate at which a given process can take place at different production stages. In Lean manufacturing, the Takt time of every production process is regulated and monitored to deliver a continuous flow.

- **Standard in-process inventory:** This is the least units of materials needed to make sure that a cell or process goes through a given speed. It's crucial that this is accurately measured because it will control several processes in the inventory without causing any downtime. A successful work standardization process provides a high-quality product and a better factory cost performance. If you reduce the variation in the shop floor, there shall be a better improvement in the productivity.

3. Organization in the Workplace: The Five S's.

One of the key tools applied in rapid development is 5s. It's the basis by which an effective lean company is founded. The 5s is the leading modular step that will assist you to discover the different types of waste elimination. The 5S are consist of five Japanese words:

- Seiri (Sort)

- Seiso (Shine and Sweep)

- Seiton (Straighten)

- Shitsuke (Standardize)

- Seiketsu (Sustain).

All these 5S generate a process for improvement.

1. **Sort**: its purpose is to make sure that items that are often required are made available and easy to identify as possible. Some of the things that aren't required regularly are discarded.

2. **Straighten (Section):** Make plans for important things so that it's easy to access. The goal is to limit the motion that is required so that workers can do their jobs. For example, a toolbox must be applied by an operator who should use different tools. In a toolbox, each tool should be located at a fixed spot so that the user can make a quick selection without spending most of the time searching for it. This kind of organization allows a user to know the kind of tools that are missing.

3. **Shine (Seiso):** It is important to maintain machines and ensure that the workstation remains clean to avoid any

problems related to uncleanliness. In certain industries, airborne dust describes a poor product service. To increase awareness of dust, specific companies paint a picture of their working environments using light colors and apply a better light scheme.

4. **Stabilize (Shitsuke):** Ensure that the first 3 S's a routine practice.

5. **Sustain:** Here you need to communicate, train, and promote the 5S to make sure that the corporate culture of the company remains alive. This might require you to assign a new team to look at the complaints in the 5S.

Once you implement it fully, the 5S' system can extend the moral, generate a positive impression on customers, and boost the efficiency of the organization. Not only will this ensure that employees feel better, but the impact on continuous improvement may reduce waste, improve quality, as well as increase the lead times. Regardless of what you select, it will increase the profit of your organization and the level of competition in the marketplace.

Going by the situation at hand, the 5S system is applied in many different ways. In many cases, it adheres to a specific plan shown below:

- Develop a plan for every "S"

- Publicly announce the program

- Organize the program committee

- Provide training and education to employees.

- Evaluate the results of 5S

- Pick a day when everyone cleans up and organizes their working area.

- Apply a corrective action.

4. Value Stream Mapping

This technique involves adding non-value added actions to produce a specific product, service, or a mix of the two. The value stream mapping is a great method to boost the status of an enterprise. It's the right technique to use to assist an individual to visualize the overall process, represent information, as well as the flow of materials. A VSM is generated using a pre-defined set of icons. The Value Stream Mapping has a common language that will explain the production process and allow sensible decisions that will enhance the stream.

A value stream map is like a blueprint to use to implement the lean manufacturing ideas. It achieves this by describing the flow of information and how materials should operate. A values stream mapping is divided into two parts. The big picture mapping and complex mapping. If you want to begin with a complex mapping, first, it's important to create an overview of the major features of the whole process.

The general picture will demonstrate how you should look at the flow, identify waste, integrate lean manufacturing principles, and display the association between information flows and physical flows.

Once you visualize the flow, you develop the ability to see where, when, and how both the information and product move inside the organization.

5. Total Preventive Maintenance

The following technique will assign a standard preventive maintenance work that comprises tightening and calibration.

Typically, TPM will assign different duties to employees to help them monitor, select, and fix the root of problems that may lead to unnecessary downtime in the machine. When you assign this specific response to the machine operators, problems dealings with maintenance are likely to take place and, therefore, you can limit the downtime of the machine. This might call for operators on a daily basis to notify the maintenance team about the machine status so that potential technical problems are realized on a timely basis.

In the TPM, the maintenance crew is one in charge of high value-added activities such as performing overhauls, deliver training, and fix problems.

A breakdown of the machine is the most important feature that deals with people on the shop floor. In addition, reliability in the shop floor is important because in case a machine fails, the entire production line may be affected. A great tool that is used in accounting for rapid machine breakdown is TPM. Below are some of the main parts of a TPM:

- **Preventive Maintenance:** This should include different types of planning on the whole device instead of performing random check-ups. The workers are supposed to do regular maintenance on equipment to detect problems. These kinds of checks help solve sudden machine failures.

- **Corrective Maintenance:** This has to do with decisions like whether you need to fix or purchase the new equipment. When you have a machine that is always down and its components keep breaking down, then it is important if you can replace those parts with new parts. Thus, the machine will last longer and its uptime will increase.

- **Maintenance Prevention**: This should include purchasing the correct machine. In case a machine gives you problems when you want to maintain, then workers will not want to perform maintenance on a daily basis, this may cause a lot of money to get lost.

6. Just in Time

The main principle of Lean is to eliminate waste. It is the most important steps when you implement Lean. Part of the process of waste elimination includes JIT. JIT is another vital feature of lean manufacturing. JIT production doesn't involve collecting a lot of raw materials, work in process, or products. JIT applies the Pull kind of system. The demand of the customer is the indicator of production. As a result, the production must be pulled out of the assembly process. The final assembly line will move to the preceding process and extract the correct amount at the right time. This process will continue as each process pulls the right parts from the preceding upstream process.

Kanban is an example of a pull-based system that has visual signals labeled using colors to send a signal upstream once inputs are sent at a downstream workstation. In practice, Kanban is a communication tool for a pull-based production.

It is similar to an information system that controls the number of parts generated in each process. Typically, there are two major categories of Kanban.

- Production Kanban

- Withdrawal Kanban

If you apply a Kanban system in the Just-in-time, the smaller sizes and big inventory reductions are realized. The JIT production, raw materials, and finished product inventory are limited. The lean manufacturing principles are applied in the clean inventory as a source of waste. Another example of waste that is removed in the JIT system is overproduction. Since each process has a speed that is not higher than that of the remaining process requirements, it's important to produce more than what is required.

7. Production Smoothing

Production leveling is referred to production smoothing because it is concerned with distributive production volumes and product mix to help fix breaks and valleys that are found in the workload. Changes that will take place have to be smoothed so that it can happen gradually and in a way that is non-disruptive. In addition, this will support the company and allow it to deal with an advanced utilization. The mixed-model technique is used to reduce the risk of products not sold, enhance quality, reduce the space, increase the demand, and control the production environment accurately.

8. Visual Management

This type of management will cause factory workers to stay informed about the status of the production plan and other crucial information that is needed to perform the job effectively. A large visual display is a great way to communicate to workers about the factory floor compared to written guidelines and reports.

When you are dealing with improvement compliance within a process, the visual representation is a better means because a team can understand a complex situation. Some of these things include the order of events, the right way of doing an action and outward relationships between actions, and other factors. Some of these tools include:

- **Visual displays**

  A visual display is made up of procedures, metrics, charts, and process documentation to reference information for worker's production. For instance, the trend for displaying performance, 100% variation of defect rate, and shipping volume status.

- **Visual control**

There are a wide variety of signals used to uphold or show actions to members in a group. This might include a release of status information and many others. For instance, the color-codes panel for temperature or speed definition to regulate the limits that allow operators to choose quickly the process that is out of the control range.

- **Visual process**

A visual process will demonstrate the correct production flow of materials. For instance, it can include a painted floor area for non-detective stock and a scrap for the right flow of materials on the factory surroundings.

9. Quality of the Source

Also called "do it right at the first time", this means that quality is important in the production process. It helps prevent defects or in case they are seen, the right action is taken.

- **In-line inspection**

The duty of quality inspection is carried out by in-line workers and not any other quality inspectors. While there are different independent quality inspectors who operate in the lean organizations, their rule should be limited because they are considered as waste in the manufacturing process.

- **Source inspection**

During source inspection, the inspectors look for defects and the causes of the defects.

- **Clear accountability among workers**

Having an inventory of partially made products provides you with a direct link between upstream processes and downstream processes. This means that the workers of an upstream process are fully responsible for the quality of the material they produce. In the same way that there is a large buffer of inventory between two production stages, the workers are also represented at the upstream process and feel accountable for any problems.

- **Poka Yoke**

It's a simple method for in-line quality testing. Sometimes it's referred to as "Poka Yoke" and is used to prevent wrong materials from entering the production process. The poka-yoke tests 100 percent of the units for the production process. These measures take place in-line by the production workers.

- **Intentional shutdowns**

Once a defect is produced, the production process is closed down until a solution is found. This is very important when you want to demonstrate a zero tolerance culture and prevent wrong products from reaching downstream to cause problems. For instance, at Toyota, any worker has a right to shut down the production line. In addition, this makes sure that accountability exists among the workers.

Other Techniques

Still, there are many other waste production tools that require a person to setup reduction, line balancing, and batch size reduction.

- **Setup reduction**

Lean manufacturing is important because it limits unnecessary downtime caused by the machine setup. Machine downtime is a main source of insignificant waste. This may require a culture of regular improvement, where every company regularly searches for a way to limit the changeover setup times.

- **Line balancing**

This is one of the best tools to use against waste. The idea is to make sure that every workstation limits the work volume that is sent to upstream workstations. This guarantees that every workstation operates in a synchronized way.

- **Batch size reduction**

Lean manufacturing focuses on the flow of materials on the factory floor. Additionally, it aims to focus on being a single piece of flow to make sure that the work-in-progress between processing stages is cut down. The smaller the size of the batch, the higher the chance that each upstream workstation will generate exactly what its customer wants and when it is required.

Chapter 3: Lean Methodology

Nowadays, information spreads very fast. It is true that we live in our world that is well advanced in terms of technology than before. Despite that, we still continue to struggle.

It is important at this moment for us to have all the tools that we need at our fingertips, but why is it that it is still hard for us to set the strategic direction of an organization? As the day closes, we seem to have drowned in a sea filled with non-relevant information. The question asked has always been how an organization can rise up and move forward?

What is the best breakthrough for a better future?

Lean processes are considered as the means for realizing process improvement. Regardless of what your organization does, it is very essential that there is some room for enhancement. Top companies use the term Lean to refer to a business methodology related to the customer and working back for the sake of making sure each step adds value.

Why is Lean Methodology Important?

Lean is among the best business methodology that anyone can apply to help cut down the cost of delivering a great service, enhance delivery, and boost the product quality. No other type of methodology can result in these benefits.

The six sigma deals with the top-down driven force to reduce costs, but usually, these gains describe a one-off and unless it is merged, they need to be sustainable. Total quality deals with quality alone. Lean, however, if it is implemented correctly, it helps managers become heroes in the eyes of the employees and customers. This will add an unprecedented level of transparency that most companies can only think of. This makes companies remain on the path that leads to more value with each activity undertaken.

To ensure that this looks more tangible, consider your personal life. Would you be okay to pay for something that was present in a different place for a better price? Some years back, these kinds of offers were not easy to find for one to review. During that time, you had to drive across town and move from store to store. But today, there are offers from eBay or Amazon that one could view in the privacy of your home. In addition, online ordering and transparency during the time of purchase and delivery process eliminate the risk of your transaction.

In your specific business life, do you think that your customers will feel the same way? All that customers want is value for their money. Lean is simply the most surefire means to show that consistency adheres and reliability exists to improve the value. All of these factors combined contribute to the general success of the business in the long run.

Maybe Lean appears like Utopian. In fact, about 30% of companies that decide to adopt Lean report success in their efforts. The other 70% that fail often fail because they were quick to give up, or because they didn't have the support from the top management to help them implement and ensure that it is sustainable. There is a big complexity to ensure that Lean can work within your firm, however, many surveys carried out show that the end will always justify the means. Additionally, the benefits outweigh the costs.

The lean processes describe the waste out of processes, to ensure that they are the best in class. A journey in Lean will never come to an end though because the overall goal is often relentless search for perfection. The lean workers never look at work as a chore. Instead, they look at the value at which they dedicate to the entire organization, this way, they spend most of their days boosting the ways of working. Leaders will allow this change by empowering and training their workers using tools to slowly and steadily enhance their means of working daily.

Chapter 4: Best Practices for Lean Development Governance

The purpose of an IT governance program is to ensure that there are mechanisms of communication, responsibility, and to support the overall enterprise strategy and goals.

You realize this by ensuring that there is a balance between risks and return on IT investments. Governance is a crucial sub-branch of IT governance. This describes the scope that deals with channeling software and system development projects. This chapter will deal with the practices that motivate the development of lean governance.

The traditional system of governance is based on command-and-control strategies that maintain and direct a project team development in the right way. This means that you are going to dedicate more work into governance effort but help accomplish little practice. The lean governance will handle a collaborative means that aims to support and inspire team members. For instance, the traditional system to guidelines in coding involved an individual creating and enforcing its application using formal inspections.

The lean methodology requires everyone to write down all guidelines, explain why it is important for everyone to adhere to the guidelines, and then organize the tooling and support to make sure that it is easy to help developers stick to the guidelines.

This section will describe the recommended methodology for governing modern software development efforts. This methodology is described because of the following reasons:

1. Experiences with existing methods to IT governance because traditional methods are very complex with a lot of advice.

2. Many project teams adhere to agile practices and these teams may be governed effectively.

3. Most teams that are yet to adopt agile practices will benefit so much from a collaborative point of view.

4. Organizations that use traditional models gain so much from "loosening the reins" depending on the methodology practice.

Overview of Lean Development Governance Practices

Familiarize with the process: Since teams are different in size, purpose, distribution, and skill set of the members, having one process is not enough. It is important to personalize the process so that you ensure that you fulfill the process to achieve the needs of the team. Additionally, it is important for processes to be examined and ensured that they are facilitated by making use of time to meet the needs of the organization.

To match HR policies with IT values: For one to hire and motivate a team of technical staff, one should have various implementations in place. It is advised to create various rewards that are key to the mindset of your members. Ensure that these rewards are delivered on time alongside other major achievements.

Mirror with the team structure and architecture: The manner in which your project team is organized is important. It is advised that the organization should represent the right architectural structure that you plan to develop.

Business-driven project pipeline: It is always a great thing to invest in projects that will spearhead the direction of the business, create some unique value, and match correctly the objectives of the organization. This specific methodology will deal with the supporting business.

Constant improvement: It's advised to highlight and learn from lessons of the whole project. For instance, a short retrospective meeting towards the end of every iteration will play a great function. It will be a huge milestone in the project.

Constant monitoring of the project: Automated metrics collection allows a person to track projects and hence select potential issues that one can work together with a team to solve early problems. You'll need to choose the least set of measurement.

Embedded compliance: It is fine to comply with your day-to-day process rather than to comply on different processes that add an unnecessary burden.

Flexible architectures: These explain the object-oriented, service-oriented, component-based, and design patterns that provide themselves with the right consistency and adaptability.

Integrated lifecycle environment: You should know how to automate most tasks like a collection of metrics. You should ensure that your tools and processes fit together in the entire lifecycle. An original investment while the project begins is by organizing all your toolset.

Iterative development: In this particular approach, the delivery of software will support continuous development and production of software components. In addition, it will encourage the release of a fine-grained adjustment and make up for a lost time.

Pragmatic governance body: A working body will provide support to development teams in a cost-effective approach and timely approach. Often, the staff is small with most members working as representatives from the governed departments.

A risk-based milestone: If you want to clear risks in your project and business. It's important that you identify a way to do this by making sure that several milestones exist in your project. The role of each milestone is to deal with a single or more task.

Scenario-driven development: It is hard to define a complete system without understanding the individual parts and the parts that are hard to define in detail if you haven't understood as a whole. When you choose a scenario-driven mechanism, you'll be able to understand how people use your system. This gives you a chance to create something that meets their needs.

Self-organizing teams: The right people to create a working plan are the ones who are going to use the same plan. Professionals in IT should respect smart people who can choose their own strategies. Once they have some guidance and a bit of coaching, they should be able to plan their work within the set parameters.

Simple metrics: These types of metrics include automation, reduced number of metrics, and understanding the reasons for collection.

A developed program delivery: This particular program describes a collection of associated projects that must be produced in increments. Rather than preventing a release, each individual should sign up to a predetermined release date. If you skip a subproject, it has to move to the next release, cut down the effect on the customers of the program.

The valued IT assets: This comprises of a programming guideline and a reusable asset like frameworks and components identified just in case an individual wants to add value to developers.

Mission and Principles

Practices that fall in this group represent a clear direction and underlying principles that will support the correct behavior. These practices include:

- Pragmatic Governance

- Staged Program Delivery

Pragmatic Governance Body

This type of program can't run independently unless there is a group of people defined to run it. The way in which a governance body organizes itself is a great determination of the general governance program. A pragmatic type of body will provide support to IT professional. This body will realize the following:

- Create an environment where people have to remain effective.

- Support a situational specific strategy, practices, and procedures.

- Support teams with an access to resources that they should have. This should comprise of a ready to access business stakeholders.

- Provide support, guidance, and mentor teams that have moved away from the normal.

Pros

This practice has two major benefits:

1. Support the spread of the right governance practices. The IT teams should adhere to the organization's governance program in case you make it simple and desirable.

2. Provide support to actionable governance. The type of governance in this situation describes a self-aware not unless the people assist in setting up and defining the processes and policies of the organization.

Trade-Offs

- **Business support:** The governance program has to describe the requirements of the business. To ensure that this is realized, it's important for stakeholders in the business to be actively involved in the governance program.

- **Needs continuous investment:** The governance body should include enough staff and since the government typically is a long-term promise, it is best for an ongoing investment.

- **Control is deployed to the executing body:** If the focus of a pragmatic governance is to allow teams, it is important for the teams to be responsible and direct them to operate within the required guidelines.

Anti-Patterns

These are some of the anti-patters that relate with governance bodies:

- **Governance for the sake of governance**: Its main focus is to ensure that there is a right documentation build by the development team.

- **Control via governance:** In this type of governance, the body will have to deal with control and instruct teams of development. You'll realize that this takes place when the governance body takes most of the time to build the procedures for the teams to adhere to.

The Recommended Default

Generate a small, medium team, often considered as a governance competency center that carriers a dotted line reporting structure to both business unit and IT.

Staged Program Delivery

Today, IT projects limit the size. The smaller projects have been considered to be successful. Similarly, an advanced business process calls for support of an advanced set of IT systems. This shows that profit generation in a business calls for an integrated implementation of projects related to similar mission and technologies. This is often realized through a management program.

A great program control has an incremental value to the business by ensuring that it is smart in the manner in which the program is staged. This will help provide a subset of all projects found in the program. Essentially, you need to break down the goals into smaller goals. The program will then support the allocation of resources and control of projects to help business goals as early as possible.

Once you define a program, the project inside the stage is regulated through a project with similar phases as the usual RUP project.

The control project will deal with the integration and support the management of milestones concerned on risk. The control project is examined by carrying out a general assessment of the entire projects. To do a risk analysis of the profile, however, combining the risk profile of every project is not enough, you'll still need to make sure that all risks associated to cross-project integration are accounted for. The control project will support coordination and flexibility when you want to implement independent projects. Iterations are the major features because it allows an organization to support projects found in a given program

Benefits

There shall be a staged program delivery, especially when you leverage a control project, support different benefits:

- **The right execution deals with business objectives:** Once you gather projects depending on the business objectives and control them as a program, you'll effectively know how to manage to deliver on important objectives.

- **A coordinated production of all the matching parts:** Using a control project with the help of a well-defined system of governance for the program through a set of milestones concerned with variance and reduction.

- **Incremental value delivery:** This divides an extensive program incrementally around a business sub-goal. When you control projects in a program through an iterative development technique, you can use new abilities if it is possible.

- **Enhanced efficiency:** A partial implementation of projects provides for a better development in different projects because this is going to provide a better tactical flexibility.

Therefore, there will be an increase in productivity. However, it is important that visible control points exist to facilitate the review of an individual project performance and the whole program.

The working of independent projects should be analyzed before the close of every iteration the moment you have a fact-based assessment.

Trade-Offs

The main trade-offs that can let in an effective staged preprogram delivery include:

- **Risk delay:** Just in case it is not handled well, it is possible for a program to affect the release date of a product. The worst case is that it will bring down the working speed of the project teams. But the truth is that it is very harsh to the company. The right way forward is to ensure that there is a correct oversight and the scope is redefined once the project fails. This implies that you can get some value delivered to the business on time.

- **Increase in coordination:** To execute a program that requires an individual to have knowledge and resources.

Anti-Patterns

The anti-pattern shown below is experienced in controlling a project pipeline based on the business value.

- **Slowest drum beat:** The slowest project will determine the pace of the general effort. The right program is linked to a train.

Recommended Default

Smaller projects are maintained in a project that is run based on the RUP's four phases.

Organization and Meetings

The type of practices that fall in this category presents a guideline to assist and determine the best organizational structure and formal reporting mechanism to handle the right stakeholders. The practices include:

- Business-Driven Project Pipeline
- Scenario-Driven Development

Business-Driven Project Pipeline

The IT needs are advanced compared to the existing resources that handle prioritization and other possible projects in the pipeline. The best kind of governance is one that improves the business value of development investments generated and ensure that there is an important alignment with the goals of the business. Also, there should be a mechanism to realize this. You can accomplish this by taking advantage of scorecards plus other control approaches that every project is compared against a set of measurements that show a strategic alignment to the business value.

It is important to understand the scorecards represent a model type of business value and each model has a disadvantage. This means that you may frequently discover that a project that has the least score is prioritized over one with a higher score. This has a habit to force manual overrides. Despite this, there are certain situations that scorecards will activate a discussion as well as the value of the business. Showing why the model isn't perfect in some cases.

Advantages

To manage a project pipeline by business value, it comes with the following advantages:

- **Convergence on the value of the business:** The pipeline management may force a company or organization to agree in the business approach and type of parameters that can send the most business value. For example, are you comfortable if your organization prioritizes new business opportunities, increases the cost efficiency of business processes, or permits quick growth of an organization?

These questions cause discussions to start based on how the projects are funded.

- **Improved ROI:** Projects that feature the best risk combination show value and alignment of strategy, producing a better ROI. The scorecards will deliver a great communication and inspirational method to the overall IT department to ensure that it remains in line with the correct strategy and optimizes the business value. If you want your project to receive some funding, it's important to ensure that you have it resemble whatever that is in your business.

- **Transparency:** In many companies, how decisions linked to funding are made isn't known. The pipeline type of management is done in an open and transparent way. This raises the level of visibility and builds on trust.

Trade-Offs

The trade-offs that you should put into consideration include:

- **Frequency:** The pipeline management has to operate on a regular basis so that projects can't be delayed. This requires for significant investment to make sure that the work is done in the correct way.

- **Released control:** This process turns out to be objective and open. It will require every project to display its business value. This may not go well with everyone, especially those who are happy with the status quo.

- **Strategy and articulation of value:** The pipeline management asks for an individual to define whatever it's that can propel investments. This is hard and it will cause you to deal with whatever it is that your strategy requires instead of your gut feeling.

Anti-Patterns

The anti-patterns defined below don't relate to the project management pipeline.

- **Game scorecard:** There are a lot of situations where the scorecards look great on paper, but the truth, they represent wrong objectives. This is performed by overemphasizing problems to make sure that "pet projects" remain on top, or by miss-scoring projects to achieve a political solution that you would like. Essentially, you need to define your scorecard until you arrive at that situation where you'll have it done right.

- **Portfolio burden:** Just in case that the process of controlling a pipeline is bureaucratic or it brings with it some time lag in the project.

- **Subjective project score:** If the project selection is subjective and unique from the others and the decisions are difficult to trace, this would mean that a poor functioning scoring process is performed without the right transparency and oversight.

Recommended default

It is better to focus on a few parameters found in the scorecard so that you can improve the business or organization.

Scenario-Driven Development

Within the practice of a Staged program delivery through project control, advanced business process should support a complex IT system and smaller projects that will allow an effective and better success rate than a big project.

You can think of the IT system as a single system that is made up of a collection of smaller parts where every part has a single system. This type of configuration is considered as a "System of Systems," where individual parts of an application are created by independent projects.

It is impossible to define the whole without having any clue of the parts and the parts can't be defined in detail when you fail to understand the whole. The kinds of risk that are here means that it is difficult to know how the parts affect the overall solution and it will drag you down when it comes to building parts that can't fit together. This happens when you apply used cases at different levels:

- Define the requirements and navigate through the used case scenarios. This requires that you reveal how the parts work together and achieve system-wide cases.

- Architecture and interfaces defined as well as traded in a similar fashion.

- Use case scenarios system. This ensures that the parts support an end-to-end of the general system.

As of today, the above technique is used successfully in the IBM Software Group. Many applications are created by hundreds of teams and customers use most of these applications.

Benefits

The scenario-driven development when it applies the system-of-systems thinking has the following benefits:

- **A better integration between parts in motion:** This will force projects that develop various applications to handle better integration between parts in motion. The main focus is on integration. This is vital because the business value is achieved through an end-to-end type of business scenario instead of an independent part.

- **Focus on delivery of business capability:** This will force every project to concentrate on the way the part delivers business value to the organization.

- **Provide control mechanisms:** The control mechanism will make sure that teams deliver the right business value. Additionally, this type of scenario-driven mechanism will help remove gaps and select any variations and areas that lack progress.

Trade-Offs

The two most crucial trade-offs linked to scenario-driven development include:

- **Business and technical vision:** This approach calls for a general business and technical vision and not many organizations have attained the right maturity level.

- **Coordination at the enterprise level:** This one depends on the potential to combine the development of various parts and not all organizations have the potential to deal with coordination at this level.

Anti-Patterns

Scenario development has the following anti-patterns:

- **IT-driven business:** Although the role of IT is to support a business process, here it is different. This will take place where there are no business processes determined or applied to support incremental IT capabilities.

- **Private visions:** The business scenarios, in this case, are loosely captured in the heads of people but never captured in a document. The end-to-end business scenario is never outlined, and hence, they can't be acted upon.

- **Ivory-tower business model:** In this type model, business processes are developed, but they aren't well produced by IT projects to support incremental IT capabilities.

- **Silo projects:** In the following example, each project will have to add a business value, but there is no release of an end-to-end business process.

Process and Measures

The previous part has described the mission and principles that guide lean governance. Additionally, it has dealt with the organization and collaboration of stakeholders for a given project. This second part will deal with the practices that revolve around processes and measures applied in Lean software development governance.

The phrase "Processes" describes the approaches used in effective Lean software development.

Processes

All practices that exist in this category improve strategies that support a project effectively. As a result, project members should support transparency and oversight when needed in Lean governance without additional overhead. The correct practices include:

- Embedded compliance
- Risk-based process
- Iterative development
- Continuous improvement
- Adapt the process

Iterative Development

Compared to the traditional software development model where all requirements are defined and stored in a single place, a team spends months to gather specs, testers receive a complete module when the cycle is about to end, and some unfinished requirements are discovered later in the cycle. Iterative development is very different and it has many great benefits.

An iterative model divides a project into different time boxes called iterations or cycles. In each cycle, it is a must to come up with requirements, perform an analysis, implement, design, and test. The sprint should include a defined set of objectives and disclose a partial implementation of the entire system. Every successful iteration generates work of the previous iterations to improve and redefine the system until it is complete.

Pros of Iterative Development

When you divide a project into several time-boxed cycles and you deliver an implemented code as part of every iteration, it is possible to achieve a few things that are related to better governance.

1. Time-boxing causes rapid decision making and a focus on what is important. If you have a deadline that lasts for two years, it's difficult to see the urgency to deliver. However, this is different if you have four weeks out deadline.
2. Fact based-governance. No matter how much you dislike it, a lot of the discussion that happens in the first two-thirds of a project is always subjective.
3. Constant delivery of a functional software will produce feedback opportunities. If you always deliver a tested code,

you may receive important feedback from the integration of various tools and key-points from stakeholders that can assist an individual to assess a functional code.

The feedback delivered is important because it will allow an individual to discover problems early and fix them. When you discover problems early, it helps save the cost of repairing the system later. If you choose the right action, you'll have the time and ability to let your project deliver a better business value.

4. Iterative development will improve the ability to build systems that can achieve the original needs of stakeholders. If you take into consideration the notion of software economics, then iterative development will provide a chance for a favorable development curve. A tested system is going to be created quickly because it has to go through different courses of corrections. This is different from a system that is far from testing. Iterative development may result in systems that meet a strategic plan.

Trade-Offs

- **Mentoring and training:** Iterative development entails an investment to retrain and support better deployment. The traditional IT experts have to go through some training to stop looking at things up front. People require to also go through some training beyond their current specialty to assist them to navigate between project activities. The business stakeholders and IT management should understand the type of input, as well as deliverables that need to be expanded at any time.

- **Project resource changes:** The techniques of iterative development require redistribution of personnel with a specific skill set. For example, testers should be available early in the lifecycle because they need to do the testing. In addition, testing should be performed in the whole lifecycle since iterative development results in difficult decisions. Similarly, architects should be called to be available because they will be important in the later stages of the project lifecycle.

- **Project management requires complex level of participation:**
  Iterative development is not an easy option to a project manager, especially in the first three-quarters of the project. This is because iterative development will force each difficult decision to be made early.
  Additionally, the project has moving parts. Instead of allowing everybody to collect requirements, after every month, it is a must to design, test, and implement the system. The only advantage is that you'll constantly avoid disappointments and problems associated with resetting expectations later in the project. The iterative ability to produce changes in a way that you manage projects for project managers and middle managers is very important,

especially when you want to produce iterative methods of developments.

Anti-Patterns

The following are some of the anti-patterns of iterative development:

- **Comprehensive planning:** Ensure that you have a comprehensive organization of the whole life-cycle, monitor the differences against a plan, and organize for the details as the project progresses. An exaggerated plan may result in total failure of the project because it interferes with the project manager from product management activities.

- **Long iterations:** Use minimum or long iterations and don't depend on feedback from the stakeholder. Why you need to apply iterative development is to help you receive a response and accommodate it faster. It is believed that once you lose the main benefits of these practices, you'll remain with less than four iterations or just a single iteration that last longer than two months.

- **Documentation-driven monitoring:** This is where you search for the status that exists in the first two-thirds of the project depending on the specification review and intermediate work products instead of analyzing the whole results.

Risk-Based Type of Milestones

Iterative development is one of the most effective approaches once it is integrated with a balance of early risk reduction and value creation. This implies that you prioritize the most critical thing to concentrate on every sprint. You can decide to create the features and represent the largest business and technical risks that deliver the best value. That said, these objectives aren't fully aligned. Hence, it will force a deliberate choice between maximizing early value creation and risk reduction.

To reduce the risk down, this may lead to uncertainty in the technology choice, this consists of commercial off the shelf choices and architectural stability alongside the mastery of the effectiveness of a team. The reduction in uncertainty may lead to variance estimations as a result of the direct link between the factors and the potential estimates.

Given that an early reduction and value creation is phenomenal for the success of a project, it is vital to have the right points in place. Remember, risk reduction should be made sure that there is a balance between the value created and running code by forcing difficult decisions that should be taken early. The precise balance for an independent project that may be different from the next one.

Significance of a risk-based milestones

These are some of the advantages of a risk-based milestone:

- **Early creation of value:** This is created by deciding on the hard choices and verifying that they are correct decisions. This will show the status of the systems as a representation of human creativity. This shows that you may have the best innovation early in the project.

- **Early loss is prevented:** Some projects are based on wrong assumptions and are bound to fail no matter what. Although most of such projects are unfortunate, you might want to avoid spending a lot of money before you realize that the project was a wrong idea. If you apply a risk-based type of iteration, you'll be able to identify projects of these kinds before you lose most of your money.

- **Increase productivity:** When you clear technical risk early in your project, it will increase how fast your projects stabilize. This paves way for a cost-effective execution since only a few technical unknowns may arise later in the project or impact the project negatively. In general, this increases productivity.

- **Reduce variance estimation**: Estimates will contain some variance and this type of variance is proportional to the risk. If you eliminate the risk early, it will mean that the variance contained in the estimates rapidly reduces.

Trade-offs

- **Adaptive process:** It resembles adaptive planning. It is important that you adapt to the process. Just in case that your processes are over-prescriptive, it will fail to deliver to the team the right flexibility that it is needed to succeed, especially during innovation stages.

- **New-planning paradigm:** Elimination of risk happens once you change the tactics depending on the type of risk that you expect. The risk-driven milestone requires an adaptive planning process that is important to get ready for the reality.

Anti-Patterns

- **Cookie cutter process:** The team is forced to adhere to a detail, prescriptive, and frequent process that offer a chance to discover risks.

- **Document-driven tracking:** In the following case, the risk is highlighted and added to a list of existing risks. These risks are then discussed by the project committee and addressed by the team. It is not a good thing to pinpoint a risk if the only thing is to complain how you don't have the right budget and time to handle it well.

- **Comprehensive planning:** The detail plans of the entire project have been generated early and allow the management to monitor the plan of the remaining project.

Adapting the Process

It's advised to adapt to the development process that requires a specific project. It's not about a process improving or less process being better. However, both accuracy and control in the project should be personalized into different factors. This should comprise of size and team distribution, amount of externally applied constraints, the stage at which the constraints are in the project, and the desire for project traceability and audibility.

Many processes typically reduce creativity. This means that you'll need to apply the least number of processes when the project is starting, especially when uncertainty exists daily in the project. On the other hand, if you start late in a project, you'll want to have more control features that will allow you to eliminate any undesired features. Additionally, you'll want to remove risks related to the introduction of late defects. This might lead to more project processes.

Thirdly, the organization has to focus on a continuous rise of processes. Perform an analysis towards the end of each iteration and the end of a project to uphold the lessons learned and adopt knowledge to enhance the process. Inspire the members of a team to search constantly for the changes to improve and deliver improvements to organizations involved in improving the process.

Benefits

When you adapt to the process it comes with various benefits:

- **Increase in productivity:** A process adapted to project requirements can either decrease or increase the production levels of a project by providing a strong integral force to the team. The end result is an increase in the effort dedicated to production. As a result, the productivity of individual members increases by showing examples and templates.

- **Repeatable results:** Processes that are adaptable will help a team to stay familiar with the requirements of the project. This ensures that a team provides the support and flexibility required to achieve repeatable results. But repeatable results can require that a person has the adaptability in the process that meets the requirements of the project.

Trade-offs

- **Requirements insights:** For one to adapt to the process in the correct way, the organization must have sufficient software engineering insights to assist in understanding whether the practice has to be used and to what level should it be applied.

- **Requires investment:** At what point should you adopt the process, you need to have some investment knowledge to make sure that the adoption and deployment are done correctly.

- **Control variations:** If you are going to let teams adapt to the process, it is going to increase the difficulty of governing a project. This is especially when you want to confirm that the correct practices are followed in the entire project. Another reason is that teams may want a unique functional product on different occasions.

Anti-Patterns

Below we list for you some of the anti-patterns associated to adapting the process.

- **A consistent and repeatable process:** Regardless of whether you apply a similar process or not, the goal should always be to deliver variability and offer room for each project to succeed.

- **More process is important:** It is important to factor in the additional process, increase documentation, and a detail up-front planning. This has to include focusing on early estimates.

- **Ad-hoc process:** In this case, you should try to create a process or adapt the process every time it fails.

Continuous Improvement

Software development is a more dynamic process. For that reason, requirements, members, and priorities of the team may change. In addition, software development has become more complex because it will deal with different conflicting problems. Given that it's dynamic and a bit complex, it is very difficult to predict correctly at the start of the project details. You may need to try, however, to be effective in software development, it is important to learn and improve the overall efficiency.

There different methods that you can apply to choose potential improvements in the software practice.

1. Informal improvement sessions

In most cases, you'll want to bring together your team and stakeholders to ask them to discuss the current status of the project. This meeting also involves a discussion of things that can be done to improve the project.

2. Retrospectives

This kind of meeting has four questions that guide it. The four questions include how something was done correctly, if we don't discuss, can we forget it? What lessons did we learn? What are some of the things that we need to change? What really surprised us? The function of a retrospective is to choose possible areas to improve.

3. Staff suggestion box

There are certain times when the easiest way to choose possible ways of improvement is by making it easy to get feedback at any time from anonymous persons. This is when the staff suggestion box becomes an important tool. It can be a physical box although most of them have been implemented electronically.

4. Editable process

This will offer the team with the right standard as well as provide them the permission and tools.

5. Personal reflection

The right habit to cultivate in your staff is to let them take time to think of how they do things, the way in which they are relating with others, and how they are realizing their goals. This kind of reflection will provide a personal strategy for improvement. Additionally, it can also provide a general improvement.

Benefits

There are different advantages that are realized with the following practice:

- **Learn as you proceed.** Teams should apply new insights in the best way possible instead of the need to wait for the following project. This may quickly increase productivity. It is the best way to integrate it with the "Develop iteratively" practice because lessons learned in a single sprint are applied in the next sprint.

- **Better control over its destiny:** This particular practice will inspire teams to carry out their own process improvement and support self-organization fast.

Trade-Offs

- **Act:** No need of selecting opportunities for improvement if you can't work on them.

- **Needs investment:** It's important to spend some time away from your project schedule and make sure that you use that time to improve activities.

- **Remain honest with yourself:** This is even more important. Many types of problems experienced by teams is a result of the members themselves and whatever that goes among themselves. It is important that you get into a project that you feel better and know that it's going to be helpful. Additionally, you should be able to pinpoint a problem regardless of whether other members will be against you or not.

- **Change your management configuration process:** Specific teams may require that you conform to a set of regulations that require one to define the process of a team. Also, the team has to validate that the process adheres to a set of conditions. The end results are that you must monitor all the changes that take place in your process, analyze the reasons for making those changes, and examine the time when the change was done to fulfill the regulations.

Anti-patterns

- **Delayed improvement:** Potential process improvement will take place towards the final round of a project. At this point, it may be late for a project to work on the selected lessons.

- **Embedded compliance:** This describes a set of regulations and corporate guidance and automated policies. The easiest type of compliance will allow an individual to achieve the right opportunity that IT experts can conform to. Despite that, to comply requires one to take important steps, especially when the work is said to be onerous by people who do extra tasks that are similar to the effort done by development teams.

Embedded Compliance

When it comes to embedded compliance, human intervention is important. Compliance is adopted in the culture when people start to know the reasons why it's important. Not everyone in the IT department should know the details, however, it is very important for them to have some knowledge of the needs of the organization to show how financial numbers are computed.

In addition, everyone shouldn't be an expert but they must be able to know that consistency is important. Once you make a choice to be compliant to the corporate culture through education, activities such as reviews become easy to perform because people will adopt compliance in their work.

Benefits

Below are some of the benefits that come with compliance:

- **Lower cost:** Once you have applied compliance in your processes, you tend to reduce the limit of achieving compliance. The manual methods of compliance may appear expensive in practice but not at all effective because people have the following habit to avoid advanced systems of compliance.

- **Less push-back from teams:** Many IT experts aren't embraced by the bureaucracy, especially one that begins from the compliance requirements. The embedded compliance makes it possible for people to perform the right thing.

- **Increased compliance levels:** Once the requirements of compliance are automated, chances are high that project teams will require to comply and produce documentation as a form of proof. For instance, to improve the traceability of requirements just in case the version control system requires individuals to check in the working product to show requirement or the type of problem selected.

Trade-Offs

There are various kinds of trade-offs associated with the embedded compliance.

- **Cultural investment:** It is very important that you spend time on creating a compliance culture inside the organization. This should include making an effort to invest in setting up a training workshop. Additionally, offer room for the development of a pragmatic guideline for people to infer.

- **Streamline the process:** First, assess the current compliance process and requirements. Look for ways that you can embed a minimum set of compliance tasks into the present software development process. It is important that you have the right knowledge and investment.

- **Tool investment:** When the time comes for you to purchase new working tools to help you automate, make sure that the tools comply with the existing process. Again, you may need to adopt the previous features into the new toolset. Therefore, you are advised to do some analysis first before proceeding with tool configuration.

Anti-Patterns

- **Documentation Inundation**
  This implies that you require to comply with an advanced priority than the need for a daily business and your

organization should begin to apply the right paperwork. Your goal has to limit the work that you require to make sure that it complies.

- **Fear-Driven compliance**
  Companies love to invest their solutions. Many of the regulations have a particular leeway to built-in. Typically, a recognition has different purposes that focus on different compliance levels. A common problem is the failure to show the front-line staff to help in the compliance. This may help limit the chances of selecting a pragmatic approach to a new mandate.

Measures

All kinds of practices included here are efficient factors to channel informed executive decision-making that will let incentives and targets. These practices include:

- Simple and relative metrics
- Continuous project tracking

Simple and Relevant Metrics

It is important to consider measurements. They direct an individual to tell how certain things are done and do them correctly. However, there are different things that you should consider before you apply metrics.

- **Metrics should be simple:** Many types of organizations decide to use metrics or avoid using it completely. This means that they are either overdoing it or failing in its application. Simple metrics have two properties. First, it is simple to organize metrics and describe it. Secondly, it should be easy to understand and describe the metrics to allow one to take action once a wrong thing happens.

- **Metrics require relevance:** Still, these organizations that collect metrics don't do much action on the results. One of the reasons for this is because metrics is not enough. For every metric, it's important to define the action to take depending on a given measure. If you can list the actions to take, then there is no need to do the measuring. Apart from that, it's important that you have the least metrics because you want to focus on the main factors.

Advantages of simple and relevant metrics

- **Painless governance:** This defines an automated collection that will limit the time and management. Simple metrics will help lower the level of complexity once you implement a manual metrics collection. This will help reduce the cost of governance.

- **Proactive governance:** The right metrics will present some heads-up just in case something wrong was to happen at an early stage compared to when you noticed it. If you identify a habit of the emergent defects, you can end up thinking that you are going to produce a low quality product at the end of the iteration. Therefore, you must know how to perform a de-scope of the features in the next iteration to make sure that you produce a better product. If you find out early about a problem, it will provide you with a choice to implement a plan to fix the defect.

- **Process improvement:** Metrics are a better means to assist an individual to know what may work and what may fail. This has a chance to produce information needed to ensure that there is an open discussion in relation to what went wrong and how one can fix the challenges in the future.

Trade-Offs

- **The number of metrics:** Once you start to collect metrics, it may be tempting to gather other types. This can look difficult and complex. However, it is better to always begin with the least metrics, then you can slowly increase the number of metrics. Remember, less is better. While you select new metrics, old metrics should be removed. Unless the cost will increase in collecting metrics and returns will also reduce.

- **Rock the boat:** Once you have collected the metrics, it may show specific truths contained in the organization that people will like to hide. If you don't have the metrics, you may not go anywhere. If this happens towards the final stages of a project, you may discover that it is doomed. This implies that you'll need to imagine the reasons or even imagine why the project wasn't successful at first.

The absence of metrics to use in the analysis will cause you to come up with excuses. However, metrics are important because they shape the objective view of what may go wrong in the following situation. In many incidences, it will prove to be an integration of things that include problems that cause an individual to deal with the organization.

- **Investments:** Metrics are available for free. So if you plan to automate the metrics, you must have an up-front investment. In case you are using manual metrics, you must have a smaller up-front investment.

- **Trust:** Metrics is an invaluable tool that you can use to get an honest discussion, to learn, and award people. It's a must to punish people just in case the metrics are bad.

- **Speak with people:** Sometimes, metrics may regularly demonstrate that there is a problem, but it will never reveal all the information that you might need so that you can deliver a great decision. It is very crucial to speak to people more often so that you can understand the actual process.

Anti-Patterns

The following are some of the anti-patterns related with metrics:

- **Metrics with no action:** Once you collect metrics and fail to take any action while the metrics achieve a particular threshold, you may have to pay for the cost of collecting metrics.

- **Documents depending on the value earned:** In the traditional system of governance, you may require to account for a particular percentage of "generated value". That represents the progress. However, the traditional value presents a false sense of security progress. The only measure of progress on software development project should include a working software.

Continuous Project Monitoring

In a continuous project monitoring, the meaning of terms is explained. You'll monitor closely the status of the IT projects in the organization through automated metrics, project reviews, and word of mouth. Many organizations have

IT projects that contain its own current status that changes in the whole project lifecycle. Projects can exist at different points and time zones. Additionally, you can have different software processes in the organization. Regardless of the challenges, every project must adhere just in case it is not well protected.

Below are different methods that can be significant in continuous project monitoring.

- **Project reviews:** A project review may include different milestones reviews. This is a periodic review that will deal with the end of the iteration and many other management indicators. This will ensure that the working code is delivered and satisfies the present stakeholders.

- **Automate measurements:** The metrics of a project that are stored through an automated means are applied in the general project. The following metrics are created and displayed by the help of a project scorecard software that will show the status of a project.

- **Verbal communication:** There are many scenarios that happen when the right approach requires one to choose the present status of a project and listen to whatever people speak. If you want to follow up a project, then it is good if you can ask a person to tell you. It's possible that metrics may indicate that something is going on, but until you confirm by asking the team, it is hard to know the truth of what is happening.

- **Post-mortem reviews:** This type of review will happen only when the project is over because the system will already have been deployed in production. Once a project is declared a success, the objective is to measure the time when the project vision is realized.

Pros

- **Fact-based governance:** If you continuously monitor projects, it is possible to base the activities on current facts. The most common problem detector has different variances from negative trends.

- **Effective governance:** This ensures that there is a correct project behavior among teams. Continuous monitoring will result in the right behavior in the entire project and not only the milestone points.

- **Early feedback:** Continuous monitoring presents early problem detection that helps a person to make the right decision quickly. This will make you receive projects that are right on time if it is necessary or even cancel them once you lose the amount.

Trade-Offs

- **It's good to select the right metrics:** You'll get whatever it's that you measure. This means that teams should understand anything that requires them to monitor the metrics and ensure that they concentrate on the things measured. This is a psychological fact that explains everything that you measure correctly. If you measure the investment and function delivered, then it turns out to be a great start because you'll take advantage of the simple metrics that define the effectiveness of a project team.

- **Be flexible:** The metrics and trends show that change is important in the entire project.

- **Warning signs are just warning signs**: Projects aren't always the same but different. There are different warning indicators that show long-term challenges that may be dealt with and other signs that may reveal a short-term level of difficulty that doesn't need governance.

- **Invest in automation:** In the short run, it is important to invest in tools to make sure that you can automatically gather metrics that you are interested in.

- **Speak with people:** The metrics indicate caution signs. They can't precisely show the type of challenges experienced by a team or deliver the information required by a team. To make sure that you control a project, you must participate actively with the team and work hand in hand with them.

Cons

- **Management of metrics:** The right actions considered to fix the challenges depend on the metrics itself and not how you understand the source of the problems. For example, imagine if the defects that a team reports increased by 57% in a single sprint. This could indicate that the team is trapped in trouble or applied the best tester.

- **Metrics deluge:** It is the most common problem associated with the automated metrics collection because you may need to collect the metrics because it is easy to do it. When you have some metrics that provide valuable information, it is important to make a comparison.

Chapter 5: Bottleneck Management

When Are You Supposed to Find a Bottleneck?

Being aware and controlling your bottleneck is an important performance measurement. However, it is important to handle big problems first. Simply because you can identify the bottleneck doesn't imply that you'll be able to select the bottleneck and has to be your greatest priority.

A lot of problems in the manufacturing industry include time, cost, and quality, and in some cases, a trade-off between the above criteria. If your greatest task includes quality and your customers return products, and then a bottleneck has the least impact on the main problems. Therefore, detection of a bottleneck as well as management may not be your biggest priority. However, it is important to fix problems that include quality.

If your biggest problem so far is the cost, then if you enhance the bottleneck, might provide some help. But before you can jump into a bottleneck detection, it is important to confirm the type of levers that affect the cost. The capacity of the bottleneck is just among the many levers that affect cost. It is important to be concerned with the most promising levers that might not exist in the bottleneck capacity.

If your major problem has to do with time, then your bottleneck might have some form of influence.

However, this depends on the incidences. Consider the lead time, it is better to reduce the inventory through the flow of material. Conversely, if you adhere to the capacity measurements, then it is good to improve the status of the bottleneck.

This should not just be for bottlenecks but for the whole. Before you make a move to change anything on the shop floor, make sure that this technique is the best to deal with the most critical problems. As for such kinds of bottlenecks, it is imagined that for the present incidence, the bottleneck management is the right option.

Overview of Bottlenecks

There are different techniques that one can use to control a bottleneck. All the approaches start with detecting a bottleneck. The graph presented below has some of the methods that one can use to improve the capacity of the bottleneck.

Boosting the speed of utilization is one of the best ways. If you choose to decouple, it may call for some extra time and money to apply. The slowest technique is to improve the capacity that will require some engineering and purchasing. However, it's still hard to understand why most folks in America begin with the slowest and expensive technical ability in the bottleneck.

What if after the improvement of the bottleneck, the system has to be verified? If it is necessary, this process should be repeated. All these methods should be available.

Selection of Bottlenecks

To sustain your bottlenecks, you need to look for the bottleneck. This is not easy, especially for a changing bottleneck contained in the production systems. If you want to change and advance a specific process that is not a bottleneck, then your system will not change.

Therefore, it is important to know the kind of bottlenecks, especially bottlenecks that keep changing and the type of methods that do and don't work in discovering a bottleneck.

Improve Bottleneck Utilization

Why is utilization the easiest technique

Bottlenecks exist in manufacturing lines. As a means to get some overview, ask the management to let you know on some of the areas they believe bottleneck exists. Most of the time, the management has the belief that they know the bottleneck and will point in areas that are suspected to exist. Well, on many occasions, the management will refer to an idle machine. The bottleneck machine isn't working.

The bottleneck process affects the whole system and becomes idle as a result of a faulty process. To ensure that you advance the bottleneck, always let the bottleneck remain idle.

This is one of the main and simple ways to improve the bottleneck. You have your device, operators, and parts. You just require to merge them. Just verify that the bottleneck is idle. The standard concept can be enhanced using extra details.

Dealing with scheduled breaks

Workers and employees like to go for breaks, whether it is scheduled and unscheduled breaks. Apart from the scheduled breaks, they also have those breaks that are caused by nature. Essentially, the machine has to go into the idle state during breaks. However, there is a chance to have scheduled breaks that will ensure that the machine continues working. For example, the first operator will break before the second operator. This means that by the time the first operator returns from breaks, the second operator will have done some tasks. Therefore, the first operator simply takes over from where the first operator left. In this case, the machine will not rest but run continuously.

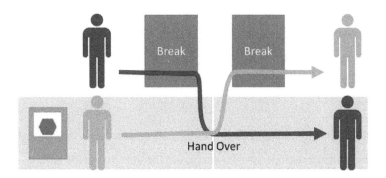

Handling unscheduled breaks

It's a bit hard to handle unscheduled breaks. An operator may require to get inside the bathroom. You can't plan for this. Thus, it's important you have another worker to be on standby. This worker should be able to fill the vacancy of the first operator when absent.

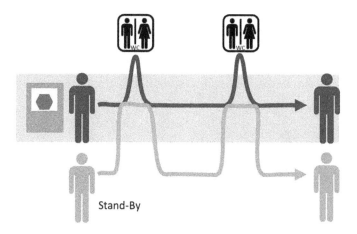

By nature, this is inefficient to have just a single operator to standby waiting until when his colleague returns. Instead, this jumper has been assigned some extra tasks that one can disrupt without leading to any problem.

Note

Before moving on to assign your shop floor supervisor with responsibilities of the toilet break coverage, remember that a team leader at the Toyota is responsible to 4 or 5 operators. In many Western countries, a shop floor supervisor manages 20-25 people. The latter is clearly unable to deal with the bathroom break besides the presence of many responsibilities.

Overtime and extra shifts

Certain methods may lead to the continuous use of the bottleneck. In theory, the machine can work for twenty-four hours a day or even seven days a week. Practically, this is low. If you are on overtime, you can decide to do additional shifts. All these may change the way you use the machine.

For advanced processes, there is a chance to fill the machine with parts before the shifts close. Once workers depart, the machine may continue to work until the remaining parts are processed or the machine stops due to some bugs.

In general, if you increase the utilization, it is usually the fastest and cheapest means to boost the bottleneck.

Improve Bottleneck Planning

Both bottleneck detection and management are crucial when you want to increase the production capacity of the system. This section will look at the effect of planning on the general production capacity.

Planning and material flow

There are many ways which the production process of a system can affect the general capacity. In the short run, you need to produce the correct products. In the long run, you can decide to level the capacity and handle seasonal bottlenecks.

Apply the pull system

One of the major factors to optimizing the application of the bottleneck is to generate the correct products. However, in the majority of the industries, the correct product can quickly change. There are some customers that may cancel orders. Other important customers might have an emergency order. Additionally, your boss may make a phone call anytime to let you know of what is important at that moment.

In other words, what might be urgent yesterday may be completely different from what is the most urgent product today. The production system has to be more agile to consider all these changes. Thus, it is important to decide as late as possible what you would like to apply as your bottleneck capacity.

Naturally, jobs will pile up in front of the bottleneck as the slowest process. In case you have a push system, your tasks will pile up in front of the bottleneck. Any form of prioritization that you might have had during the time when the job was added to the system will be gone already.

Thus, in a push system, you are more likely to generate the wrong products with the least priority. Use a pull system to manage bottlenecks. In general, all manufacturing system will benefit highly from a pull system. Besides this, there are important advantages once you select the priority and only when the system has the potential to work.

In case the pull system will deliver a product that should be stocked through Kanban alone, it is going to be self-poetizing. If you release some custom-made products to order, then that means that you can't keep them in stock. In this situation, Kanban is just a signal that comes, you have to select the most urgent job from the entire list of available tasks.

Apply the correct pull system

If you are using a Kanban system, then already you are through with the first hurdle with bottlenecks. But in case the bottleneck does not change much, it is possible to fine tune the system. If you have multiple processes that add up to your system, then there are many ways you can set up the Kanban loops.

For instance, a system that has three processes, you'll have four options to choose if you want to loop the Kanban. But for the case of a bottleneck, it is important to decide as late as possible what you want to produce. If a signal comes from the customer, it is advised to get the signal to the bottleneck in the most direct way possible, as well as get the product to the customer as fast as possible.

Lot sizes

This can also affect the application of the bottleneck. In general, if the lot size is smaller, the closer you can follow the customer demand. By nature, if your changeover time isn't zero, you might not want to change often. However, you need not to change over too rarely as you generate the wrong goods.

Seasonality

Most of the industries have a seasonal customer demand. During these occasions of the year, the demand is often high but low at times. Demand usually heightens in fall and early winter when people want to purchase their gear for the coming winter season.

Decoupling bottleneck

Based on their nature, bottleneck change. Small bottlenecks will shift. The bigger the buffer, the less likely that the bottleneck will shift. Therefore, you can boost your system capacity by adding more buffers before and after the largest bottleneck.

Obviously, this will also be a trade-off. Through decoupling, you will increase the inventory and response level of the system becomes sluggish. However, here is a little trick. Based on their nature, buffers that are outside the bottleneck are often full. This means that you receive all the negative effects that come with an increase in the inventory.

On the other hand, the buffers that come after the bottleneck are often empty. They fill up once the actual decoupling toward a downstream process is required. Therefore, you will receive all the advantages of decoupling, but just a few of the drawbacks, you will need to have the space ready to contain the parts. As a result, the buffer after the bottleneck might be preferable to buffer before the bottleneck.

Despite this, you aren't supposed to drop your buffer before the bottleneck to zero. Otherwise, the bottleneck may lose efficiency. Another reason is that decoupling the bottleneck doesn't imply that you don't have other buffers required in the system. In case you just buffer your bottleneck and nothing happens, possibilities exist that interactions between other processes may impact the biggest bottleneck frequently. Therefore, it is a great practice to ensure that you have some buffer between stations.

Capacity Improvements

Perform an update or install new machines

Lastly, if you want to boost your system performance, then you must increase the capacity of the bottleneck. Most of the time, this includes performing an update of the existing machines. For some reasons, this slow and expensive method is often the first one that is chosen by many companies. Instead of improving the free utilization, or even adjust the planning with little effort, or spend time and effort to decouple, most the companies will go out and request an expensive machine.

Well, this is not only slow and expensive but very risky. Just in case you didn't identify the bottleneck, you may have installed extra capacity without benefiting the system.

Identify bottleneck using value stream mapping

When it comes to identifying bottlenecks in software development, that is also another area that many companies and individuals have a problem. Many developers ask themselves where could bottlenecks be? While you might be familiar with some of the common bottleneck such as if it takes about 5 hours for a build to end. However, this may not be the biggest bottleneck in the whole flow of generating value for your customers. Although it might take

5 hours for a build to end, does that mean that it will take about a week for the code to reach the production stage?

A value stream map refers to a tool that a person uses to evaluate processes and highlight bottleneck, improvement opportunities, and waste. Choosing the biggest bottlenecks in a specific process stream is the place where value stream mapping excels.

Advantages of value stream mapping

To select bottleneck is one of the most obvious advantages of value stream mapping. It will allow the whole organization to identify the biggest bottleneck and how it negatively affects the value. If we apply the previous example, we might say that if you are only aware of the 5-hour build time, chances are that you might be tempted to concentrate your effort on enhancing that alone. In case you don't know the significant bottleneck, then the following week of deployment, if you decide to enhance the build time, it will likely cause the downstream bottleneck to be much worse. However, if everyone in the organization can understand the biggest bottleneck, then it means the organization will concentrate on limiting the delay to the benefit of everyone, most importantly customers.

Getting Started With Value Stream Mapping

The steps of a values stream are simple:

1. Highlight the steps of the whole process. Keep it simple by labeling the most key scenario via the process.

2. Gather data. Record the mean time taken to finish each step and the average wait time between every step.

3. Build a simple flow diagram that describes the "value add" times for every step and the "wait times" between every step.

4. Select the biggest delay in the flow and find out why the delay is as long as it is. Next, generate a plan to limit the delay and work on it.

Common Problems

At one point, every business must have gone through an application development bottleneck. Efforts applied in the development of an application can't match with the demand in the business. Therefore, business users stuck around waiting for applications. This section will review some of the most common problems that contribute to bottleneck and some of the methods that you can address them.

A great question for you:
Do you think the application development efforts by developers and programmer live up to the demand in your company? When your users and customers ask for a solution, how long do they take to receive a reply?

Delays are one of the main causes of problems in different kinds of business. Development lags pull behind demand and the users have no choice but to wait for weeks or even months before they can receive new solutions.

What is the end result of this type of bottleneck in development? Generally, it is always painful and it hurts the business in different ways. The first thing is that it impacts the productivity of the business. Certain users will get tired of waiting around and find their own solutions, without disclosing to the IT department.

That means, if your business is trapped by a bottleneck in the development sector, you have two questions to respond to: Why is it happening and how can you better fix it? Below are some of the possible things that may trigger application development bottleneck.

Lack of detail in the requirements

Have you made an attempt to explain to your friend something only for them to understand a different thing? These people will often interrupt whatever it is that you were saying with something that is completely opposite.

This will happen, especially in the software development industry. It is the leading challenges that many software developers experience. Developers have a difficult task to understand the requirements of the users. Most don't understand exactly what the users want the system to look. In some software companies, it operates like a conveyor belt where requirements pass through the hands of many people before reaching the developer's table. This means that by the time the developer receives the requirement document, a lot of changes have been done such that important notes from the users aren't captured. In this case, the developer has no option but to develop a solution based on what is written in the requirement document. The end result is a system that is different from what the user asked for. The user has no option but to reject the system and return it back to the developer.

As this happens, remaining projects that the developer was responsible continue to be delayed.

Well, how better can such kind of problem be handled? One way is to give developers enough time to interact with the users who want a specific system developed. The developer should get the chance to listen to the requirements of the user before they start to work on the project. A face-to-face interaction between the developer and users gives the developer an added advantage to hear from the user. They have a chance to ask for clarification of anything that may not have been clear. Once the project development starts, it's important that any progress is shown to users to look at and give feedback. This should be the second method that will make sure that the correct system is built instead of wasting time.

More details in the requirements

On the flips side, more detail in the requirements may trigger a bottleneck. In any kind of development, the Pareto principle will apply. According to this particular principle, just 20 percent of the features solve 80 percent of the problems. In many occasions, the features that require a lot of effort deliver the least value.

However, users remain blind about how long every feature may take before it is implemented. In fact, what may appear as a simple feature may take days before it is developed.

There are users who are just ambitious when they write down requirements. These users will ensure that they list all the features but don't rank it based on significance. This then adds days, weeks, and months to the development project. In this case, the developer assumes that all the features listed are important. To find a solution to these kinds of problems, it is good to discuss with the users and give them the list to rank the features based on which is very important. If you can do this, you will have a great idea of where you can start in your development plan.

Quality assurance is done at the end

In each development project, you'll experience many incidences where things aren't going to be fine. There are times when requirements will be lost during the process of translation. This means that the final product will fail to fulfill the needs of the users.

Other times, the users are presented with a working system and reject it because that is not what they wanted. Or it may exactly be what they asked for but not what they wanted. Sometimes, users go to use the end product and discover that it doesn't work. Maybe, there is a small bug in the system that keeps preventing the system from working.

So, what can one do when some of these problems arise? In most cases, the application goes back to the developer for more rework. This means that the length of the project increases and this will affect other projects that the developer was currently working on. The final result is a development bottleneck in the organization.

Well, how can an individual fix this kind of problem before they become worse? The answer is to allow users to take part from the start until the point when the product is released. In addition, apply a quality assurance process early in the project. This will allow you to handle all these kinds of problems before they affect other projects.

Over-dependency on a single department

Typically, a business will go through a development bottleneck because a single department gets overworked. Usually, there could be minimum hours in a day to complete a project.

For example, a development project that goes through an IT department. However, this department also handles hardware, reporting, and many others. It becomes hard for this kind of department to dedicate most of their time to finish projects. Besides, if the business doesn't want to increase the number of their staff, then it is going to be hard to avoid development bottlenecks.

To limit the number of bottlenecks, look for tasks that the company can delegate to other people within the organization. For example, a Business Intelligence and reporting tool is a form of IT burden. But with the advent of self-service BI tools for reporting, these are now tasks that can be done by end users. While it is different depending on the type of company, many similar tasks like the one mentioned help free an IT department.

The most important thing is to ensure that you have a higher access to end-user tools. To cut down on the development bottleneck, it is also important to deliver to users the right tools that they can use to accomplish most of their tasks on their own.

1. Technical debt

Does your company have a legacy system? It is normal to run on systems that are outdated because they are important to your business to continue to remain active. To replace these kinds of systems, there are some additional costs that you may have to agree and come with a plan to deal with it.

However, these systems may fail to match exactly with the current world. A modern application may not operate well with old systems. Or your legacy systems aren't filled with a lot of spaghetti code, that any change you make could affect other related parts of the systems.

The challenge is that each application you build has to be integrated with this system. This kind of integration isn't just time-consuming, but also adds complexity to the system.

Solving Bottlenecks

The greatest challenge with software product development has to do with visualizing the work so that you can identify where there are delays in the process of changing ideas from "concept to cash".

Making work visible

The first step involves ensuring the work remains visible. In the knowledge work like software development, it is hard to identify the work that is being done, which is a visualization approach like Kanban. Below is a view of a Kanban board.

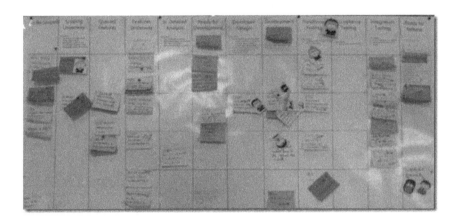

The Kanban board is an important "moment in time" view, but it is hard to easily identify patterns that may develop over time. If you consider the Kanban board in particular, does it make it easy to respond to these questions?

- For how long have been work items been waiting in the above column?

- What is the approximate time for work items in these stages to be complete?

- How often do you see queues in this step?

- Are the queues a special event or it simply happens regularly?

Visualize the work overtime to understand the queues better

If you build a cumulative flow diagram, it will increase the visibility that there are consistent queues of work in the functional testing and acceptance testing process over time. The queues are represented as bubbles that rise in the cumulative flow diagram.

Can detective work indicate the causes of queues?

The functional testing requires someone other than the person who builds the functionality to validate that it is okay. In other words, this is a test to ensure that it is free of errors. Once the functional testing is complete, then the acceptance testing phase is carried out by a business analyst or product manager.

Chapter 6: Deliver Fast

"Deliver fast" is a major principle of Lean Software development and everyone likes that it is a great thing to do. Nobody wants to deliver slow. The only challenge is how can you go about doing it. At one time, a Scrum Master once asked a developer, "How can I deliver fast?"

Well, the answer is simple. If you want to deliver fast, you have to ensure that your whole team thinks and deliver fast. Thinking small describes different aspects of Agile development. The three factors include:

1. Smaller units of work

2. Less work in progress

3. Maximizing throughput and not utilization

We shall look at these factors later on.

As a developer, you'll not like the idea of a software sitting on the shelf. Perhaps waiting for weeks before it is deployed. Most developers want to see their finished piece of code channeled into production as soon as possible. You probably want to get feedback from users about the usability of a specific technique or whether users are finding it interesting to use a particular functionality that consumed most of your time.

The only time that developers know how their code reacts and how users interact with a particular feature is when it is deployed.

Therefore, if you increase the delivery process, you'll be amplifying the learning process. A fast delivery helps eliminate the possibility for the creation of incomplete assumptions.

Besides the needs of a developer to get the code into the production process leads to many benefits, most importantly, allows the client and organization to have a reasonable time frame. The clients standing on the receiving end of new features, which must solve problems for them and the business can generate money from such changes.

With time, the requirements continue to change. Thus, if they aren't released, the requirements keep changing depending on the business assumptions of the business analysts or product owner. Developers want the changes in requirements to appear depending on the kind of feedback from clients who apply the function in production.

While a month is a long time to wait for requirements to be delivered into the production, 1-2 percent change in requirement is more tolerable than a quarter of your requirements changing in a period of a year.

The 80:20 rule seems to work on requirements. In most cases, 80 percent of value is realized by 20 percent of the features. Therefore, get the 20 percent out very fast. More often, you will realize that many features present aren't needed. So by increasing the speed of development, you seem to validate the requirements and remove unnecessary work.

As a developer, nothing is worse than the need to support a piece of functionality when it is channeled into production weeks or even months since it was completed. One of the reasons is that developers forget some of the things that they implemented. That is why it is important for them to get feedback early so that in case things don't run well, there should be no strain to remember whatever you did.

To achieve this, it is necessary for developers to include practices and infrastructure in place to ensure that there is fast delivery as often as possible into the production. If you need to go through some steps in order to deploy, then you need to do one every day. You need to ensure that you can activate a build and deploy at a click of a button. This will remove waste and reduce the risk by having a repeatable process. Humans make errors, but machines don't. Instead, they perform each instruction that tells them to do. Additionally, machines can do it fast.

It is also important for developers to get into a habit of looking at the quality of the produced code every time. Suppose the developer is working on a large project, which may not be done before the next release, then they need to toggle their code with toggle features. This calls for effort and foresight on the side of the developer, but there are several benefits.

The application of toggle features permits a complete deployment of incomplete features into the production. The feature toggle will allow for the dark launching of features that one can apply later on. There are also some additional benefits such as the potential to "switch off" a piece of code that has been released recently if it is defective or not working the way it was expected.

To deliver the code into production as often as possible removes the traditional, manual methodology to quality assurance. Make sure that testing is automated from the automated unit tests to automated acceptance tests. Once you have teams of "testers" running manual regression test packs isn't economically possible.

The role of a tester in Lean or Agile team keeps changing. If you consider the traditional waterfall project, testing used to be a quality measure that had to be done before moving into the next step. When a project is delivered at a high cadence, then the role of the tester has to be moved to the start of the change to help in the identification of missed scenarios.

The culture of the organization is important to change so that there can be fast delivery. Organizations that have a hierarchical structure and depend on waterfall development methodology will fight to move towards a rapid deployment. This is the time when shifting to the development model proves useful. A very great principle, "you build it, you run it". This methodology results in a long-term view and builds on "product teams" rather than "project teams". Teams learn how to collaborate and their choices are channeled towards a long-term, rather than the duration of a project.

Creating the potential and the ability to deliver fast cannot happen in a single day. There are a lot of practices and tools that should be present for a team to operate at its optimal point. Top of which exists Test Driven Development, Continuous Delivery, and

Continuous Integration. Apart from tooling and practices, the organizational culture should evolve to allow this to take place.

How to Deliver Fast by Thinking Small

Let's now get back to the three aspects of Agile development.

1. Smaller units of work

It is important to ensure that you have smaller units of work that can easily be generated in a single sprint. In case your stories are very big, you can divide them up. There are different techniques to help break up stories. Some of those techniques include:

- CRUD: This represents Create, Read, Update, and Delete. The four main operations that take place on a data object are key to dividing a story.

- The steps of a workflow: In case a story has numerous steps in a workflow, you can decide to break down the story into individual steps.

- Acceptance criteria: In case a story has most of the acceptance criteria, you can decide to apply the acceptance criteria as a guide to split the story.

- ANDS, ORS, and Commas: If you have a story that has many acceptance criteria, you can apply that acceptance as a means to split the story.

- Happy Path First. Exceptions Later: If you add all the exceptional cases to a story, it will make the story large, try and divide the main "happy" path into its own story, and add the exceptions later into the stories.

- Supported Technology Platforms: In case the functionality of your story has to run on numerous target platforms, you can attempt to split the story based on the platform and target the most frequent platform.

The splitting techniques are so many, these are just a few that you can apply. The best-known technique of splitting is Bill Wake's "Twenty ways to split stories"

Caution

Sometimes it is very tempting to split stories based on task or by architectural layer. It is not advised to use either of these approaches and not many people apply them. If you split stories using this approach, it does concentrate on delivering a complete and production ready piece of usable software with every story. Therefore, neither of the above approaches can deliver value to every story. There is no business value in the design or UI because the user can't interact with it or offer feedback on it. Just like the saying, "You can eat half a fully baked cake, but you can't eat a half-baked cake."

2. Less work in Progress

This is another technique that you can apply to assist in quick delivery and help reduce your team's Work in Progress (WIP). Most of the times, you'll see teams that struggle to ensure stories reach the Done column at the end of each sprint, and in most cases, many stories are in progress. The major reason why high WIP levels might lead to slower progress is that it attempts to generate multi-tasking on the side of the team members.

Instead of including many in-progress stories that move from one sprint to another, concentrate on less work progress stories and aim to ensure that they reach the Done. There are different tricks that you can apply to try this:

1. You can set the WIP limits and not begin with new stories till it reaches the in-progress ones and gets done.

2. Once you plan a sprint, make sure that you plan out the order of when the stories shall be worked on and delivered within the sprint.

Performing either of the following will allow your team to work together and ensure that work is done sooner.

3. Optimize the throughput and not the utilization

When you limit the WIP, you'll at times experience a lower utilization of individuals. That is fine. It is fine. Don't forget that the goal is to ensure that you have more work product out the door faster and not ensuring that each person is at 100% utilization. The best analogy is to make use of everyone at 100%+. What happens to a freeway when it is at 100% capacity? The same thing will happen to teams. You can imagine freeways. Here are some similarities between freeways and teams.

1. The actual rate at which a freeway can slowdown increases rapidly as utilization increases. The traffic will reduce faster at 80-90%.

2. Once the traffic incidents happen, the effect is even higher during times of increased utilization.

3. If a freeway is at or attains a maximum capacity, its potential to deal with the unexpected decreases quickly.

The above principles still apply to software teams especially the third item. There are different unknowns and random events that will happen. As a result, it is important to ensure that plans get a higher slack to account for these. If you decide to focus on the highest utilization, teams will begin to fall when things blow out. What would be the result? The throughput of the team will actually slow down. Thus, to "deliver fast", you must ensure that you concentrate on the work and ensure that the work is done instead on keeping the team membership busy.

How to Think in Lean to Boost Delivery?

Agile practices have a tendency to build a system that will limit waste by carefully handling the end-to-end work processes. A system that describes a whole value stream map that allows team members to visualize all the steps. The size of work in the queue definitely describes the relationship in the work in progress, hence organizations can enhance operations by limiting the lead time. This will also include the whole team in generating the value stream mapping plus the developer can build products and services that impress the customer. If you apply Lean Kanban principles in the portfolio selection of product initiatives, it will assist in waste elimination because leaders check and prioritize initiatives when they perform a selection. Typically, the organization will create and apply a single product backlog. Integrate development teams into smaller groups to offer a better balance between processes improvements and value delivery of products.

Chapter 7: Design Thinking with Lean

These days, the business language has been highly improved with the methodologies and philosophies that have gained popularity throughout the past years. Design thinking, Lean Startup, and Agile. More and more companies have continued to accept the numerous chances and benefits over the business performance delivered by the use of these methodologies in the whole process.

Despite these, just understanding these methodologies and the benefits it brings in the entire implementations is not enough. As with anything that exists in life, the more choices we have, the harder it becomes to generate sense out of everything. Intelligently prioritize what is going to work best at every moment and under explicit cases. When applied in software development surrounding, the largest portfolio of processes, tools, and methods from design thinking, Agile and Lean Startup deliver unlimited chances when combined and exploited.

At first glance, this may be considered as incompatible, by just applying the above approaches during the development of numerous projects. It is believed that each of them will contribute to the creation of its own way. Once teams remain open to understand and embrace these practices, the complementary value becomes known.

Well, what is the basic foundation of every methodology and how are they different and similar? How can they fit together to realize a final outcome and which part of the innovation stage do they develop the biggest effect and offer the highest substantial value?

Blending Lean, Agile and Design Thinking

Typically, disciplines are very different because of the application of different cadences, with a lot of practices and vocabularies that deal with successful measures.

An engineering team that makes use of Agile should be focused on delivering a bug-free code regularly. The main thing is an increase in velocity at every sprint. Product managers that decide to use Lean are often interested in building efficiency, waste reduction, and tactical background.

Don't forget that designers decide to apply customer front and focus on verifying a problem solution that fits the Design Thinking activities. However, there are activities such as design exercises that are said to be time-consuming and slow down the production of a new code. Each discipline is going to operate through its own techniques and this may aim at an ideal state of success that is unique to them. This type of collaboration shared some understanding and improved productivity.

Does this imply that every discipline should operate in any manner that is best for them? No. Without having a clear understanding of the customer, especially when it comes to Design Thinking, engineers will concentrate on shipping the features without having any sense of whether they have solved the customer need.

With the availability of different practices, inspirations, and metrics of success, it is the main reason why companies may find it difficult to integrate the processes and produce a highly productive and balanced team.

Work in short cycles

Can you imagine if you could understand how people may respond to a specific change? This resembles making an assumption that can predict the final state of each software. That is pretty hard.

Since it is difficult to tell how people might respond to a given change, making this assumption is very risky. To reduce the risk that comes with implementing the changes that fail, perform small steps. This is one of the main aspects of Lean and Agile. Pick an idea and attempt it with a small team. Show the following practice as a "Process Experiment". Let them perform some trials and allow them to see how it comes out. If it fails, this should be a sign to the team to invest little time and effort to this kind of change. However, if it is successful, the team has a responsibility to uphold a practice, improve it, and the organization should also deliver it.

Perform daily retrospectives

Retrospectives are the center of a continuous improvement. It is one of the most common type approaches that is used in Agile. The main thing about retrospectives is that it provides a team with an opportunity to consider the present practice, analyze the efficiency, and discover how to progress. Teams that successfully hold a retrospective realize improvements.

Before the end of each cycle, motivate your teams so that they can meet, review everything that has gone well in each cycle, what failed, and commit yourself to improve one or two things. Sometimes, this may appear dull but teams will start to open up and speak about the major issues that they are going through. If things don't work, let the teams have an external facilitator conduct these particular retrospectives. A person who has nothing to lose will do well in a retrospective to pinpoint the root causes.

Do minimum research and more often

User research has been in existence for some time and is one of the most important tools in the design teams. Regardless of what you are going to test, you must have a two days interval.

It is important to always look for a competent moderator and have a great testing script. This will help you review each issue within the first testing aspects. For each aspect, you'll receive limited value.

User research is important. One is advised to do it with the help of a cross-functional team. However, the most important thing to consider is to do less all the time. Instead of testing 12 participants, just test three. Pick the learning from those three and then do your best efforts to test it again in the following week. Make sure that you don't get lost. Just progress with working in the office to ensure that you have a maximum participation. The most important thing is that you must display your findings once you complete the test. Show the value of the exercise, reduce the commitment of every participant.

Work as a balanced Team

The major tool to use to plan the team. The team in this case is made up of software engineers, designers, and product managers. As you can see, the team doesn't have an "engineering team" or "design team" at any level of the project. A balanced team should comprise of experts and generate perspectives that are important features of a project.

Once it is organized in the above way, there is no point to train different members of the team. No difference exists in the cadence of engineering design or the product management of the balanced teams. It is important for the efforts to match and be aligned with the goal of delivery.

Prioritize product discovery and work equally

One thing that happens with many organizations is that the work visualized is the work done. Agile, in particular, presents a clear image, practices, and approaches around work visualization. This is one the reasons why organizations that use agile have a specific type of physical boards or monitors.

Agile provides support to a continuous learning. Similar to Lean, Design Thinking focuses on learning. However, there are no open approaches or practices linked to work visualization. The delivery features of agile include visualization, measurement, and implementation. Therefore, Agile emerges as the winner because of the design thinking activities. The final result of this work doesn't receive the same treatment as the delivery work. But it shows the efforts and provides room for it to be cut in case a scope crunch takes place. Typically, team members should be asked to track their time and energy on delivery.

To avoid this, the work of product discovery should be first in the backlog. It has to be visualized alongside with the delivery tasks. Thus, it is important for one to monitor the delivery tasks and the impacts of the discovery work should be seriously considered. In most cases, learning will uncover the gaps that exist in the backlog or poor decisions made. The process of changing plans with respect to this learning is called agility. That is the reason why you should apply this type of working and is the main factor behind the creation of a responsive team and organization.

Review the incentive structure

This is a crucial factor to allow your teams to select the best productive mix of the three philosophies. Teams will have to optimize the tasks that they are incentivized to accomplish. That means if you induce the velocity, the team will have the duty to work on more features. Therefore, if you create enticements in learning, it will make the teams create better products.

The same technique should be applied in the performance scale of the company management criteria. If you want to generate a collaboration and learn, it is very important if you assess employees depending on their efficiency and ability to create a continuous learning into their work. For example, speed is only rewarded when a user shows satisfaction in the features shipped. Incentives like these are very popular with agile teams. By understanding that their organization places emphasis on the values of their behaviors inspires teams to determine the kind of Agile, Design Thinking, and Lean that will allow them to find help.

Chapter 8: Technical Debt

What is Technical Debt?

There are certain problems experienced in code that are like a financial debt. That is according to Ward Cunningham, one of the Agile Manifesto authors. He further said that it is fine to borrow against the future, as long you ensure that you pay it off.

Since the time Ward used this metaphor, it has increasingly gained popularity. Although there are disagreements about the correct definition of technical debt, the main concept identifies a sequence of the problem that most software teams struggle to control.

Ward applied this term during the time when he was building a financial application in Smalltalk. His purpose was to prove to his boss the kind of refactoring that they were performing, for that reason, she adopted a financial analogy.

Ward said that if you don't succeed in making a program align with whatever that you understood to be correct means to think about the financial objects, then you will continue to face a disagreement that is similar to paying interest on a loan.

Why use the term technical debt?

The idea of technical debt is a great means to communicate the needs for refactoring and enhancing tasks associated with the source code and its architecture. If you can do an estimate of the time required to fix whatever that is not correct into your code, the concept of debt, then you can draw a comparison to other data projects.

What technical debt includes

A wrong type of code may have many errors and issues. This means that this could be related to the structure, architecture, test coverage, documentation, possible bugs, code smells, coding practices, and style. All these issues affect technical debt because it has a negative effect on productivity.

Technical debt might arise during the life of a project. As time moves on, you might understand something new concerning the application domain. You can now consider your initial architecture when you receive a technical debt.

Do we have other types of debt?

Not all software project problems are a technical debt. For example:

- Identified defects are not technical debts. But it is a quality debt.

- Wrong or delayed features are not technical debts but a feature debt.

- The absence of skills isn't a technical debt but a skilled debt.

- Poor processes aren't a technical debt but a process debt.

Is technical debt a bad thing?

Taking a shortcut to release a product on the market so that it can deliver the right business value is probably not a bad thing. However, it is important for a person to be conscious that the Technical Debt incurred might hurt sooner or later.

At some moment, the team should try to pay back at least some part of the accumulated Technical debt. They are various ways that you can achieve that, and there is no piece of magic that can suit all situations. For you to fully understand the incidence and accomplish the correct strategy, Technical Debt has to be analyzed and transparent.

How can you analyze technical debt?

Not all Technical Debt items are the same. For you to understand the incidence, it is crucial that you analyze them.

Ways you can handle technical debt in the codebase

Regardless of what you are talking about, "debt" seems to be one of those dirty phrases to use. There is a good reason for that, this is similar to the unrestricted form of spending that may lead to kinds of financial woes, software development approaches that may generate a bloated codebase that might be handled by Band-Aids.

If you do your own research, you will come across many different definitions and talks about what a technical debt is made up of, but this will always come to a common point of agreement. Technical debt is one of the most unfortunate issues experienced in software shops.

There are many causes of Technical Debt, right from a sloppy kind of development to an organizational apathy. Well, how can individually handle the pressure and numerous other factors that result into a technical debt? Experts suggest two ways of dealing with Technical Debt, one is to pay it back and prevent it ever happening in the first place. In both incidences, success depends on the composition of culture and process and the whole organization.

Manage and Repay Technical Debt

If it is leveraged correctly, technical debt can be a crucial tool for ensuring that there are realities and business objectives. Many people wouldn't be able to purchase a house or car without getting some loan, but the people who do it right have a method to pay back the debt. The same principle applies in software. If you are very careful about your code, then you might never commit a line of it. If you make a reasonable amount of technical debt and have a plan to pay it back in the future, it could be important in the success of the general product and organization.

There are occasions when technical debt could be tolerated for the sake of the business. Incidences happen where ivory teams generate beautiful architected and designed software months when the market window is already closed.

Regardless of that, even organizations that place a strict value on the software quality experience some "technical debt". To tame technical debt, it is important to have the right management and repay the debt. Below are some expert tips for doing that:

1. Don't hide technical debt under the rug

If you pretend not to see a stack of bills on your desk, that doesn't mean that you don't owe the cash. The worst technique to technical debt is chosen to bury your head in the proverbial sand. Never should you ignore the technical debt or considered a taboo or issues with the engineer. Instead, it is important to embrace the debt as a chance to make the system better. One approach you can apply to reduce technical debt include is to remain proactive about choosing new debt in the code as it is generated.

2. Execute processes and methodologies that are useful

The correct processes and development methodologies are essential to manage and reduce technical debt. The correct combination of development processes should involve the ability to decide on your technical debt instead of having it happen by accident or failing to know that it is accumulating. These frameworks may include some variations like:

- Transparency of the business on whatever it is that they are buying for every release against what they are placing on the technical debt.

- The concept of rapid improvement so that there are a formal means that you can enhance the state of things in case the technical debt isn't well managed.

- A processor framework that will force re-factoring.

- The idea of a "Definition of Done" that teams use to define a possible release candidate.

- Providing technical teams a seat at the table when they prioritize work. This will allow technical team to be part of the coming release.

Frameworks, processes, and methodologies create the right environment to face technical debt. One of the most common theme in the advice given related to technical debt is to avoid moving a new debt into a certain bug-tracking graveyard that no one has some bucks to work on or track.

Prevent Technical Debt

Sometimes, the best medicine is to prevent. This is never easy but has some benefits. To avoid triggering technical debt, below are some tips:

1. Cultivate the culture of quality

Teams that are designed based on the culture of a comprehensive software are more often to prevent technical debt from emerging. And once it arises, it is more likely to be serious when it comes to paying it back later.

To prevent technical debt is a side effect of creating a culture that places emphasis on quality. Once everybody starts to care about producing a quality software, technical debt is going to be prevented. This type of culture has to move throughout the org chart, from junior developer to senior developer and above. It has to allow hiring, processes, and workflows as well as performance incentives.

2. Educate non-technical stakeholders on realities

Any developer is aware that the "ship it now" pressure in the organization can be real and especially when a patchwork solution finds its way out of the codebase credit card. That is why it is important to have an open, honest conversation about a technical debt with non-technical members.

No matter the picture of your company, to educate stakeholders concerning a technical debt is and why they are supposed to pay attention to it. This will make them understand as well as appreciate the needs of communicating the business impact of technical debt in business terms that are specific to a given business.

3. Implement processes and methodologies that will help

There are different processes and practices that will allow one to embrace the culture of quality and prevent technical debt from taking place. Some of them include accurate, automated tests that change in the code, develop and adhere to a set of coding standards, performing code reviews and pair programming, and adhering to a well-defined QA process.

Chapter 9: Automated Testing

Proofing for a mistake is an important concept in Lean. It is the major thing when it comes to the release of a quality product and eliminating waste. This is very true in software development because of the manufacturing. Automated testing is a main method of mistake-proofing in software development.

In the same way, automated testing is very important in agile methodologies. It is a ubiquitous approach in the agile development industry that is assumed that nobody can write a new piece of code without performing a few automated tests. Although this is false when it comes to legacy code, there has been a surge of automated testing applications.

This is a wide topic, in this chapter, we refer to all kinds of testing. That includes performance testing, behavior driven testing, integration testing, and many more.

Every type of testing has a particular focus, but all share the following features:

- Developers generate tests manually
- Test harness run tests
- Tests can run automatically without any interruption
- The developer is aware if something goes wrong

Lean software development requires automated testing. It is very important because it helps:

- Build quality
- Eliminate waste
- Creates knowledge

With automated testing, wastes in the systems are identified and removed immediately. Therefore, there will be no room for defects to find its way into the system in the later stages of development. Since automated testing eliminates these form of wastes, it helps save cost.

Automated testing mainly supports the creation of quality. A codebase is made up of a set of automated tests that self-check and self-validate. This is vital because it will reduce the chances that unnoticed error sleep into the system.

Lastly, automated tests work as evidence to demonstrate the way you can use APIs of the codebase. This is vital because it helps create a firsthand knowledge that developers and programmers must trust.

Why Test?

There are several advantages that come when you choose to perform automated testing in your system. Below are some of the benefits:

Productivity and quality

The quickest way to improve your productivity and quality of software is to make sure that you have a complete suite of automated tests. Most developers achieve this through personal experiences and independent studies.

For any moment that a project lacks a suite of automated tests, developers get cautious about executing the changes especially when they aren't familiar with the code. This means that in many occasions, they will spend time learning the code that is going to be changed and study the application of the code in the entire codebase. Up to this point, developers feel like there is something important that they have missed. This may add extra time to the process of development of new features.

In case your project contains a suite of automated tests, it will act like a safety net for programmers. Rather than spending most of their time learning and understanding the target code, the programmer can decide to implement a great feature that is easy to understand.

Once become confident to add more changes to the code without performing any additional research, you'll save a big amount of time. In addition, since problems are identified and corrected instantly, you decide to delete any complex and costly rework that might occur in case the problems are detected later in the project cycle.

Finally, if a developer gets interested to learn how a piece of code works, they will not rely on a detail documentation because based on experience, it has been shown that this particular type of documentation is outdated and wrong. That is why developers should study the code itself. The tests will explain how the parts of the code can be used and how they can be proved to be correct and up-to-date by applying them.

What is Automated Testing?

It is important to know what automated testing is and what it is not. For that reason, it is not running tests that are created automatically or generated by software that scans and does an analysis of the code. Although you may refer to this as automated testing, it is not the type of testing that we are referring to in this case. In the automated testing, the focus is on checking the correct behavior of the code, something that tools that analyze code can't perform.

Automated testing will guarantee the ability to implement a set of tests at the touch of a button. These tests are created manually, often by the same developers who develop the code that is tested. Typically, the boilerplate code that will represent the skeleton of a test will automatically be produced instead of the initial code itself.

Test Harness and Test Suites

A test suite describes a set of related tests. The tests in a suite are implemented, one at a time, by a piece of software referred to as a test harness. There is a lot of freely available, open source test harness. The most popular is the xUnit. A specific test harness is often specific to a given programming language or environment.

While the test harness cycles move through the tests it is going, it will essentially perform several things. Before it runs all the individual test, the test harness will ask the test suite's setup routine to perform an initialization of the environment where the test will be run. The next thing, it has to run the tests and the test harness will record information about the success or failure of a test. Lastly, the harness will ask the suite's down teardown routine to clean up the test faster.

The test harness will then display the results of all the tests back to the starter of the tests. There are times when this may be a console log, however, the test harness is triggered by a GUI application that will show the results graphically.

In the graphical interface, when the tests run, you will see a green progress bar that shall move toward the 100% once every test is finished. This progress bar will remain green as long as the tests succeed. On the other hand, if the tests fail, the progress bar will immediately turn red and remain red even when other tests are run.

Chapter 10: Tips on Lean Software Development

Elimination of waste originates from uncovering a software system or its specifics. It is all about discovering what the customer wants and delivering exactly what they asked for. This means that you don't spend any time trying to implement a functionality that the customer didn't ask for because the client won't like that.

Trim the fat using Lean software development

The term lean has been in existence for quite some time now, but the concept of lean goes way back. Lean principles have some origin in the Japanese roots. The strong focus of lean is on efficient use of available resources. This is an important idea in the whole development journey of Lean software development. The manufacturing and automobile industry is perhaps the most popular areas where people relate the lean philosophy because Toyota made an initiative of marketing basing on this particular philosophy of Lean.

Interpret Lean

There are different means that a business can adopt lean methodology. One way is by choosing to eliminate waste. If you decide to start from the idea that any resource applied in the production has the ability to be wasted, you may easily start to look for areas where there is a leakage of resource. Then you can begin to plug holes there. This particular idea is similar to the sustainability initiatives because you can decide to apply it anywhere. However, tangible things aren't just the only area of focus. Some activities that don't match up with the final objective for a customer can be seen as a waste in the system. Therefore, the management style and capital allocation may easily come under strict focus once an organization decides to go lean.

The second method to adopt lean is referred to as "mean". This works based on the principle that wastefulness emerges because you are doing it wrong. This method narrows down on each area where poor quality is identified as the source of waste. This may involve individuals being held accountable for wrong choices, selecting an outdated process that people have stuck with, or even highlighting an end result that is failing to deliver its promise. Think of this approach like the first step to coming out of addiction. First, you must accept that there is a problem before you can begin to look for methods to help you get better. It is very hard to apply this particular approach of Lean management if you haven't stepped on some toes, but the end result may be justified.

Lean concepts shift into the tech sector

Similar to Scrum has taken over the software industry and is applied in an enterprise project, lean principles have filtered into the IT industry. The lean software development is a method that integrates well with other agile methodologies. For instance, one way in which this technique works to eliminate waste is by emphasizing on a clear set of requirements for software. That is a field where Scrum is usually weak. That means when you combine the best practices from both approaches, you might end up with a strong outcome.

How you can go lean in your next software project

1. Eliminate waste: This is all about identifying the exact needs of the customer and working towards delivering those needs alone.

2. Keep your choices open: Don't rush and decide too early about how you should accomplish a given goal or build your entire method around the idea. This may easily render you unproductive if you don't remain careful. Instead, try to concentrate on building a process that is open-ended to support last minute changes and improvements. This way, you'll be able to deliver a quality product by adopting some of the lessons that you have learned along the way rather than going back to the first step.

3. Educate the customer and let the customer educate you: The iterative method of software development will let you demonstrate to the customer what you have so far. This way, the customer will have the chance to highlight any inconsistency between whatever it is that they were thinking and what they said they wanted and what you heard. Given that, to go lean requires the provision of value like the way the customer looks at it. This type of feedback is critical.

4. Everyone should cooperate and take responsibility: It's hard to go lean if there is a big resistance from members and managers in the organization. It is important that everybody plays an active role in ensuring that each sprint cycle is successful. Speed originates from a team that is committed to take initiative and ensures that things are done. If not, you'll be stuck with bureaucracy, hierarchical systems that will limit your efforts of going lean.

5. Never ignore quality: Lean software development requires that all aspects are working well as promised. This is easy to notice if you are implementing agile techniques that might place finishing a

product first before getting it right. If you have to spend more time and resources on testing, LEAN recommends that you do that. That is how you touch the heart of the customer. Don't forget that in the current fast-moving world, people will never forget when you deliver a product of lower quality. That is why it is advised that you focus mostly on quality.

Lean tools in software

Create a continuous-one-piece flow. In the traditional methods of manufacturing, cost was reduced by producing large parts at the same time. In contrast, if you optimize a single part of the process, generates inefficiencies and a general decrease in flow. Lean advocates for delivery of a single part.

Limit work in progress

To ensure that you get a single piece flow, you must remove multitasking. Thus, developers are advised to work on one thing at a time. Well, the question comes in when developers want to hand over work but the testers are still busy?

Develop a pull system

Rather than push work to the next step in the chain, how about pulling it. This requires testers not to accept work until when they are ready. The developers in this case can't pull work, even though it will affect the work in progress limits. They have to think about how they can assist the testers. The only way is to test themselves maybe by writing test tools or drivers. Instead of looking for a bottleneck and complain about it, you can decide to pull systems to expose the bottleneck and fix it, therefore, you will increase the throughput.

Improve the work area to remove needless movements

The best example is that of a worker walking a few feet to pick a letter, organize it into five bins, and repeat the entire process for a whole list of mail. Instead, you can bring all the work items into one central place and sort without walking.

In software, objects are somehow different, compilers, frameworks, databases and version control. However, the truth is the same. Many programmers have their code on various environments, with build systems that take so much time.

Limit scrap

A great example of this one is to decrease the amount of defects that disappear into production. If you can, you should also prevent it from reaching the tester. Still, if a tester encounters a defect, they have no option but to stop, reproduce the problem.

Backlog Management

What is backlog management?

This is the process by which the owner of the product adds, modifies, and prioritizes backlog items inside the backlog to ensure that the most valuable product is shipped.

If you have an oversized product backlog, it becomes a challenge. It will affect innovation. Additionally, it will also slow down the time in the market. Thus, this will cause more frustration even when you have the best Agile teams. This section will look at some of the challenges of having an oversized backlog and how you can fix it.

Challenges that come with backlog management

In the agile development set up, the major tool to use to control the roadmap and build predictability is the backlog. However, as it grows uncontrollably, the value that it generates decreases.

When you have a very long backlog, it becomes a root source of pain to most agile teams. By virtue of the sheer level of information, it will be unmanageable and irrelevant. It will then be left behind. Teams will switch to reactivate sprint planning. As a result, they will lose sight of the long-term set goals and find themselves in a task-focused surrounding. Because it is easy for one to think about what needs to be done now than what you can do in the future.

An overly massive backlog has its own challenges

Maintenance costs: Blindness to queues is a reality. Queues lead to more cost, where every item will continuously call for attention for it to remain valid. Building a fat backlog may look like a very big task that means that it is omitted. Finally, this will cause the entire backlog to become obsolete.

Reduction of value: Every product in the backlog of tens of thousands of products will appear insignificant. If you add a new item, it will appear pointless. In case backlogs get very big, they will become a trash bin where you drop all the work that you want to do.

Inhibited innovation: To reorganize a big backlog takes time and is very tiresome. As a result, great ideas are added at the front or towards the end of the backlog. If you place items at the start, you are simply invalidating the rest of the backlog, while you adding them towards the end means that it will never be done.

Why is that the size of backlogs gets too big?

With the following problems in mind, we can look at what causes backlog become oversize. The truth is that there is no just single reason or cause, but it's a combination.

Hoarding: By nature, humans are born hoarders. We have a hard time to throw away anything, especially brilliant ideas. The goal of maintaining the backlog is not to know what should flow in, but decide what should flow out.

Information needed: There is this kind of belief that keeping an eye on everything at a granular level provides one with a great idea about the scope. However, just like responding to changes is important in agile and lean software development, the further in the future we have plans, the less certain they are. Therefore, granularity should emulate that.

Dependency solution: When you aren't truly agile, you'll struggle to resolve dependencies far into the future. To select dependency chains, you have to break down large items into their components to help you limit the goals into tasks. This causes a double-negative effect on backlog quality. First, it will build the backlog balloon. Secondly, it implies that the backlog will not all be value-driven, and instead, heavily focused on what kind of work to do.

Making Backlog Lean

Below are some tips to use to improve the size of your backlog.

1. **Take seriously the role of the product owner**

This should have one person, no more, no less, that should be accountable for the backlog at each sprint. Essentially, this person should be accountable for a single team backlog as well. This person should be accorded with enough time to maintain the backlog together with the team and external stakeholders. The person must be knowledgeable about the product and develop authority to make important decisions inside the backlog without including other parties.

2. Limit the design process

A great starting point is to begin at the Design in Process inventory. What you should do here is to set a limit to show how many items that can be in the backlog. There is no single size that fits all. However, the best starting point would be a size per product owner(PO). Because a PO is often accountable for a backlog, the capacity of a PO to oversee the information is the limitation point.

3. Make a decision on how to manage the backlog

Develop a simple and open strategy of how you want to control your backlog and involve your team in the process. The product owner holds the key to maintain the backlog, but they are not the only ones to contribute to the vision. Everyone on the team has the responsibility to contribute and regularly participate in the process of ensuring that the backlog remains fresh. For this to work, everyone is supposed to have a basic understanding of backlog because this is the vision of the product.

4. Make decisions

Learn to restrain yourself from every idea that pop up in your mind, keep it in your head and if it continues to remain there after a week, it will be worth to backlog.

5. Work with an aging idea

It is possible for a product backlog and a team backlog to be divided into different stages where the design in process limit may be more difficult the nearer they are to implementation. The easiest approach would be to commit one portion of the backlog to new ideas and another portion that is well groomed and restricted in size. Provide the ideas in an age limit so that the ones that aren't prioritized disappear over time to avoid flooding this part. Once the idea is moved into the following part, it will show a commitment from the PO that this concept will be implemented eventually.

Conclusion

Lean software development processes have been widely applied all over the world. This is because it is the best approach when you want to eliminate waste in software development. It is accepted by the world for rapid development. If you focus on the solution that Lean methodology generates, it will help eliminate waste in the system and your software development process can be productive. In this book, you should have come to the conclusion that lean software development is one of the best methods for one to use when it comes to the elimination of waste in the product. Additionally, it helps in early detection of waste and improves the project visualization. Once the waste is identified, the priority is accorded to how it can be eliminated plus its causes. Causes may include extra code, partially done work, and many others.

Lean methodology is best for new startup organizations and new entrepreneurs that want to handle new projects and avoid unnecessary delay in early processes.

Since the current enterprise solution is complex, the so-called lean practices which are adaptable to change and responsive are best for software development. However, it is important for organizations and IT companies to factor in which Lean methods are important to the company or specific projects.

If you think you learned something valuable via this book, please do leave a review on Amazon, it will be much appreciated.

Wish you the best of luck in your development endeavors!

www.ingramcontent.com/pod-product-compliance
Lightning Source LLC
Chambersburg PA
CBHW051055050326
40690CB00006B/727